"The foolishness of the world sometimes feels overwhelming. *The Wisdom Pyramid* lifts that fog away, revealing just how full God's world is with goodness, truth, and beauty. By turning to these sources, in proper order, the wise will find folly fading into the background, and the world will look like—and be—a different place. Wisdom, as this book reminds us, is right there in front of us if only we will turn our eyes upon it."

Karen Swallow Prior, author, *On Reading Well: Finding the Good Life through Great Books*

"One of the most important books I've read this year! What if you woke up to discover you'd been eating only Doritos and Oreos for a year? When it comes to our 'information diet,' *The Wisdom Pyramid* reveals most of us essentially have been consuming junk food—with an ensuing onslaught of personal and public health crises. McCracken is like a doctor who not only diagnoses the source of our cultural malady with precision but also prescribes the cure: a change in how we consume knowledge that can promote healthy wisdom and love of God."

Joshua Ryan Butler, Pastor, Redemption Church, Tempe, Arizona; author, *The Skeletons in God's Closet* and *The Pursuing God*

"Brett McCracken's *The Wisdom Pyramid* models the discernment he asks readers to practice. Thoroughly biblical, it is also informed by a wide range of sources of truth, beauty, and goodness. From Augustine to Jacques Ellul, Reformed theology to pop music, historic Christian hymns to modern poetry, McCracken models how to wade through our daily deluge of input, form unhurried habits of attention, and grow into the patience and humility of godly wisdom. I imagine this book becoming essential reading for families, student groups, and churches."

Jen Pollock Michel, author, *Surprised by Paradox* and *Teach Us to Want*

"It has been said that 'we make our tools, and then our tools make us.' Engaging a wide cross section of insightful analyses, Brett McCracken offers profound wisdom about how we have more information, less truth, and a shrinking capacity for identifying truth. Well-informed, vividly illustrated, and aimed toward solid answers, *The Wisdom Pyramid* is a must-read."

Michael Horton, J. Gresham Machen Professor of Systematic Theology and Apologetics, Westminster Seminary California

"The first time I discovered Brett McCracken's wisdom pyramid diagram, I knew he was onto something. I used it the next Sunday. Lots of people talk about it. Why? Because Christians desperately need a balanced diet of information. This book is amazingly helpful at both diagnosing a problem in contemporary Christianity and offering a holistic solution. *The Wisdom Pyramid* is clarifying and convicting. It's a must-read guidebook for discipleship in our information-saturated age."

Mark Vroegop, Lead Pastor, College Park Church, Indianapolis; author, *Dark Clouds, Deep Mercy* and *Weep with Me*

"In an age of perpetual distraction, hurried commentary, and shallow conclusions, we're quickly losing our aptitude and appetite for wisdom. Brett McCracken's book is a much needed antidote for the dangerous ethos of the day. A compelling call to reorder our lives and reorient our hearts and minds around the shape of biblical wisdom—loving, listening, and looking to God—*The Wisdom Pyramid* is essential reading for anyone who longs for a more meaningful journey of faith."

Jay Y. Kim, Lead Pastor of Teaching, WestGate Church, San Jose, California; author, *Analog Church*

"The digital revolution has transformed—not tweaked—the fabric of daily life. Never has it been easier to gain attention, or discover entertainment, or obtain knowledge. No wonder we're addicted. But Google is a pitiful substitute for wisdom. Indeed, if we're not careful, life online will make us aware of everything and wise about nothing. That's why I'm so excited for Brett McCracken's antidote to the inverted priorities of our age. If you live on an island without WiFi, pick a different book. Otherwise, *The Wisdom Pyramid* is for you. Few things reinvigorate the soul, after all, like exchanging the stultifying air of a Twitter timeline for the fresh sea breeze of an excellent book. And this is an excellent book."

Matt Smethurst, Managing Editor, The Gospel Coalition; author, *Deacons* and *Before You Open Your Bible*

"It is genuinely disturbing to consider how we are being shaped by our current forms of information intake. Brett McCracken's *The Wisdom Pyramid* is a godsend—a pathway back to sanity and health. I believe that the proposal offered in *The Wisdom Pyramid* is as important for our mental and spiritual health in the modern world as a proper diet is to our physical health. On top of that, this book is beautifully written, winsome, actionable, and hopeful. Buy a copy for yourself and lots more to give away!"

Gavin Ortlund, Senior Pastor, First Baptist Church of Ojai; author, *Finding the Right Hills to Die On*

"As a mother, I want my four children to develop the habits they need for a life of wisdom. They are quickly growing up into adults who will have to navigate for themselves the constant clicks and pings of life in our global, digital, information age. And so, I want their childhoods and teenage years—and our family life as a whole—to be intentionally formed by things that are both true and lovely. Although it's not specifically a parenting book, *The Wisdom Pyramid* is a gift to parents, giving readers the essential tools to establish habits and priorities for a life of wisdom. This is a helpful book, and it's also a hopeful book. It's helpful because Brett McCracken writes biblically and insightfully on every page. It's hopeful because it ultimately reveals the wise life to be the very good life."

Megan Hill, author, *Praying Together* and *A Place to Belong*; Editor, The Gospel Coalition

"In an age of post-truth and information overload where Christians are constantly persuaded by AI algorithms and anecdotal absolutes, Brett McCracken winsomely pushes us past verified checkmarks and Facebook fact-checkers to bring us to the God who sits over wisdom and truth."

Thomas J. Terry, Director, Humble Beast; member, Beautiful Eulogy; Lead Pastor, Trinity Church of Portland

THE WISDOM PYRAMID

THE WISDOM PYRAMID

Feeding Your Soul in a
Post-Truth World

BRETT McCRACKEN

CROSSWAY®

WHEATON, ILLINOIS

The Wisdom Pyramid: Feeding Your Soul in a Post-Truth World

Copyright © 2021 by Brett McCracken

Published by Crossway
      1300 Crescent Street
      Wheaton, Illinois 60187

Cover Image & Design: Phil Borst

First printing 2021

Printed in the United States of America

Trade paperback ISBN: 978-1-4335-6959-3
ePub ISBN: 978-1-4335-6962-3
PDF ISBN: 978-1-4335-6960-9
Mobipocket ISBN: 978-1-4335-6961-6

Library of Congress Cataloging-in-Publication Data

Names: McCracken, Brett, 1982- author.
Title: The wisdom pyramid : feeding your soul in a post-truth world / Brett McCracken.
Description: Wheaton, Illinois : Crossway, [2021] | Includes bibliographical references and index.
Identifiers: LCCN 2020030246 (print) | LCCN 2020030247 (ebook) | ISBN 9781433569593 (trade paperback) | ISBN 9781433569609 (pdf) | ISBN 9781433569616 (mobi) | ISBN 9781433569623 (epub)
Subjects: LCSH: Christian life.
Classification: LCC BV4501.3 .M3314 2021 (print) | LCC BV4501.3 (ebook) | DDC 248.4—dc23
LC record available at https://lccn.loc.gov/2020030246
LC ebook record available at https://lccn.loc.gov/2020030247

Crossway is a publishing ministry of Good News Publishers.

VP   30   29   28   27   26   25   24   23   22   21
15   14   13   12   11   10   9   8   7   6   5   4   3   2   1

To Jeff McCracken, who taught me to love wisdom

CONTENTS

Introduction

AN UNWISE AGE

Wisdom cries aloud in the street,
  in the markets she raises her voice;
at the head of the noisy streets she cries out;
  at the entrance of the city gates she speaks:
"How long, O simple ones, will you love being simple?
How long will scoffers delight in their scoffing
  and fools hate knowledge?" PROVERBS 1:20-22

OUR WORLD HAS MORE and more information, but less and less wisdom. More data; less clarity. More stimulation; less synthesis. More distraction; less stillness. More pontificating; less pondering. More opinion; less research. More speaking; less listening. More to look at; less to see. More amusements; less joy.

There is more, but we are less. And we all feel it.

We have vertigo from the barrage coming at us from every direction, every day. We are nauseous from the Tilt-a-Whirl nature of a constantly changing, always unstable world described in (often contradictory and whiplash-inducing) feeds of fragmented and partisan news. Our ears are bleeding from the screeching multitudes who daily assault our senses. Everyone has a megaphone, but no one has a filter.

Our eyes are strained, brains overstimulated, and souls weary. We're living in an epistemological crisis. It's hard to know if anything can be reliably known. We are resigned to a new normal where the choice seems to be: trust everything or trust nothing. Or maybe the choice is: trust nothing or trust only in yourself—a seemingly logical strategy, but one that sadly only inflames our epistemological sickness.

How can one flourish in a world like this? How can one fortify one's immunity and be healthy amidst a contagion of foolishness whose spread shows no sign of stopping? How can Christians become storehouses of wisdom in this era when more and more sickly people will be looking for a cure?

Better Habits of Information Intake

This book proposes that we need a better diet of knowledge and better habits of information intake. To become wise in the information age—where opinions, soundbites, diversions, and distractions are abundant, but wisdom is scarce—we need to be more discerning about what we consume. We need a diet comprised of lasting, reliable sources of wisdom rather than the fleeting, untrustworthy information that bombards us today; a diet heavy on what fosters wisdom and low on what fosters folly.

You might remember the old "Food Pyramid" from your childhood. First published in the US by the Department of Agriculture in 1992, the Food Pyramid was designed to help people understand the folly of eating only french fries, soda, and candy—and the wisdom of eating grains, fruits, and vegetables. The Food Pyramid was a brilliant visual guide for healthy eating habits, offering guidance for how many servings of each food group helped form a balanced diet.

We need something similar for our habits of information intake. We need guidance for how to daily navigate the glut of information available to us, an ordering framework for navigating the noise and the mess of our cultural moment. We need a "Wisdom Pyramid."

But before we get to the pyramid's practical guidance for "eating" well in the information age (part two of this book), we first need to understand the nature and sources of our sickness (part one). How did we get here?

The New "Post-Truth" Normal

The 2020 COVID-19 pandemic exposed the severity of the epistemological crisis we face in the digital age. As the new virus spread globally, public health experts and government leaders naturally struggled to understand the nature of the contagion and how best to contain it. But the speed with which information—good, bad, and ugly—spreads in today's world meant that imperfect data, errant projections, hastily written analysis, and contradictory recommendations were spread confidently and quickly, resulting in a disaster of information every bit as dangerous as the disease itself. Whatever you wanted to believe about the pandemic and the "stay at home" restrictions issued by governments, there were articles, studies, and experts you could find online to defend your view. The result was a deepening cynicism and uncertainty about pretty much everything.

COVID-19 didn't create these frightening information dynamics, but it was a crisis made worse because of them. It was really 2016 when the extent of our epistemological crisis became apparent. That was the year Donald Trump's election to president in the US and "Brexit" in the UK stunned experts and accelerated feelings that the world was entering a new, unpredictable phase driven more by rage than reality, more by fear than facts.

As a result, Oxford Dictionaries declared "post-truth" the international word of the year in 2016, defined as "relating to or denoting circumstances in which objective facts are less influential in shaping public opinion than appeals to emotion and personal belief."[1] The new "post-truth" normal was underscored in early 2017 when *Time* posed the question, "Is Truth Dead?" on its cover, designed in such a way to mirror a *Time* cover from 50 years earlier which posed a more foundational question: "Is God Dead?"[2] These two covers, a half century apart, tell an important story. Without God as an ultimate standard of truth, all we have are "truths" as interpreted by individuals. *To each their own. You do you.* It's no wonder we are now as confused as we are. Do away with God, and you do away with truth.

Our Mental and Spiritual Sickness

I recently spoke to a group of college students and asked them two questions. First: "How many of you have a smartphone?" All forty hands in the room went up. Second: "How many of you would say your smartphone has made you a better, happier, healthier person?" Three hands went up.

Generation Z, or *iGen* as psychologist Jean Twenge has dubbed them, are living their lives through phones. And they are not happier. With lives characterized by ever-present screen time, texting, and social media, iGen has subsequently been defined by rising rates of depression, loneliness, anxiety, sleeplessness, and suicidal ideation.

"It's not an exaggeration to describe iGen as being on the brink of the worst mental-health crisis in decades," wrote Twenge,[3] who assembled a vast array of research to support this thesis in her 2017 book *iGen: Why Today's Super-Connected Kids Are Growing Up Less Rebellious, More Tolerant, Less Happy—and Completely Unprepared for Adulthood—and What That Means for the Rest of Us.* The title says it all.

Twenge shows in her book how rising rates of mental-health challenges among iGen started spiking in the years following the debut of the iPhone in 2007. The lines on various mental illness graphs became steeper when smartphones became ubiquitous. Surely that is not a coincidence. And it's not just iGen who is increasingly sick from the toxins of our digital age. Mental illness is rising across the board. The number of Americans diagnosed with major depression has risen by 33 percent since 2013, as shown in a report from Blue Cross Blue Shield in 2018.[4] Though rates are rising most rapidly among teenagers, every age group is seeing a rise. And it's not just an American problem. Depression is now the leading cause of disability worldwide, with over 300 million people suffering from it across the globe.[5]

Research also shows Americans are increasingly unhappy. The year 2017 marked a new high in unhappiness in America, according to the Gallup-Sharecare "Well-Being Index." A record twenty-one states saw their well-being scores decline in 2017, and for the first time in nine years no state's score improved by a statistically significant margin over the prior year.[6]

People are also increasingly lonely. Cigna's "2018 U.S. Loneliness Index" found that just under half (46 percent) of Americans always or sometimes feel alone, with the highest levels of loneliness among Generation Z and Millennials. Loneliness "has the same impact on mortality as smoking 15 cigarettes a day, making it even more dangerous than obesity"[7] and is increasingly regarded as a public health crisis by governments around the world. In 2017 the UK became the first government to appoint a "Minister for Loneliness," followed by a comprehensive, £21.8 million "loneliness strategy" to address the crisis.[8]

Our cultural sickness in the digital age is real and growing, and there are signs it is affecting our physical health too. After increasing for most of the last sixty years, US life expectancies started decreasing after 2014 and are still on the decline—largely due to rising rates of suicide and drug overdose.[9] But statistics, national surveys, and well-being indexes are one thing. The day-to-day, experiential realities of living in this diseased environment are another. To some degree or another we all feel infected.

Nausea, Addiction, and Other Ailments

I feel the sickness constantly. When I open Twitter and see the latest array of vile name-calling, self-righteous ranting, and virtue-signaling, I get squeamish. When I find myself meandering on my phone—scrolling through Instagram, clicking random links, checking sports scores, or whatever—I often feel removed from my body, lost in a digital rabbit hole. Even as I write this chapter, the phone on my desk has lured me into its web probably a dozen times. Why? How do I stop this? How do I resist checking my phone first thing in the morning, last thing at night, and multiple times each hour in between? The questions trouble my mind, as they probably do yours.

The sickness I feel—which so many people feel—is akin to that of the slot machine addict. We've been conditioned in a Pavlovian way to keep putting proverbial coins in the machine. The dings and flashes of our push notifications give us dopamine hits that keep us hooked, as they were engineered to do. We want to see who pinged us, what people are saying about our photos, and what's getting the mobs riled up today. It's terrible for us, and we know it, but like other vices—alcohol, tobacco, sugar—it's addictive.

There are other symptoms I experience. I find myself skim-reading books now, or I find myself reading a few pages of a book, then something on Wikipedia, then a few more pages of the book, then

Twitter, and so forth. Then there is the headache-inducing anxiety of response-demanding notifications—the never-ending pings from text messages, Facebook messages, Twitter, Instagram, WhatsApp, Slack, Voxer, MarcoPolo, Asana, LinkedIn, email, and various others. It's the feeling of swimming upstream and never making progress.

These and other ailments prompted me to write this book. Having experienced the sickness in myself and seeing it in others, I want to champion a better way—a way to be sane and centered and virtuous in this crazy world. I want us to be discerning in an age of distraction. But before we get to the medicine, we must first understand the causes of the sickness.

Three Habits Making Us Sick

We must examine our daily diet of knowledge intake. It can be nutritious, making us wise and shrewd, more able to ward off intellectual infections and spiritual afflictions. But it can also be toxic, making us unwise and more susceptible to the lies and snares of our age.

Below are three poor habits of informational "eating" that are particularly prevalent in today's world, habits contributing to our sickness. The next three chapters will examine each of these poor habits in more depth, but here they are in brief.

1. EATING TOO MUCH

Just as eating too much of anything makes us sick—stomachaches, indigestion, or worse—too much information makes us sick. And nothing characterizes the Internet age quite like "information overload."

Have a question about the Bible? Google it, and there are hundreds of answers. Need a video tutorial for how to install curtains? There are tons of them on YouTube. (Trust me, I watched at least five of them.) Looking for the best croissant in Paris? Try searching Yelp, TripAdvisor, or countless other websites that have an opinion.

In theory, the vast repository of information at our disposal is a wonderful thing. In practice it's often paralyzing. Even with Google's algorithmic "ranking" of search results, it's overwhelming to sift through the glut. For example, every mommy blogger and baby-whispering guru has a different recommendation for sleep training. Whom do you trust? Whose method actually works? The lure of the all-knowing Internet promises to clarify, but often it just complicates.

It's the problem of limitless space. Whereas physical stores and communities are bound by limitations—a supermarket can only stock so many brands of coffee, and a family only has so many opinions about what to cook for Thanksgiving—the Internet does not have any of those limitations. For coffee, Thanksgiving recipes, and anything else, the options are extensive. Again, in theory, it's freeing! In practice, it's frustrating. How do you choose the best option among so many that are undifferentiated, untested, and—aside from user-submitted reviews—unvetted?

The "limitless space" nature of online media has also created a situation where "news" channels must find content to fill 24 hours a day, seven days a week, resulting in a diminishment of what qualifies as "newsworthy" (e.g., filling an hour with live car chases). On the Web, not only is there the expectation of daily, fresh, "breaking news" content, but there is fierce competition for clicks. Desperate to stand out, websites are motivated to use incendiary headlines and other tricks to collect coveted clicks by any means necessary. The result is content that is often rushed (a hot take on yesterday's controversy), random, reckless, or even distorted to spark short-term controversy rather than long-term wisdom.

In the competitive landscape of the digital age, the "food" of information is not getting more nutritious; it's veering in the direction of junk food. Doritos and Skittles will always get more clicks than spinach. And so we walk down the buffet line of social media snacks and online junk food, daily gorging ourselves to the point of gluttony. Unsurprisingly, it is making us sick.

2. EATING TOO FAST

When you inhale food in a rush you often pay for it later. However convenient it may be, "fast" food is generally not the most nutritious. Most of the best food, both in nutritional value and overall taste, is prepared and eaten slowly. As with food, so it is with information.

We live in a harried age. Events that dominated headlines one week are forgotten the next. Social media favors what is #Trending at any given moment but has no incentive to circle back to last month's societal conundrum, let alone last year's. The Internet is a medium of *now*. Its memory is short; its shape ever changing. To navigate life online is to always be playing catch up: reading the article everyone is sharing on Facebook, following someone's Instagram story before it disappears. If you don't respond to your friend's text within 20 minutes you might jeopardize the friendship. If you are a "thought leader" and you don't weigh in on the social media outrage of the day, you might lose your thought-leader status. Whether in hot-take clickbait or well-timed Twitter threads, fortune favors the fast on the Internet. It doesn't favor wisdom.

Such a pace has no time for critical thinking. When we are conditioned to move quickly from tweet to tweet, hot take to hot take, it's all we can do to skim the thing, let alone read it with careful, critical thought. Scholars have found that the "junk food" nature of information intake online is rewiring our brains, such that our cognitive abilities to think carefully and critically are being eroded. "In a culture that rewards immediacy, ease, and efficiency," writes literacy advocate Maryanne Wolf, "the demanding time and effort involved in developing all the aspects of critical thought make it an increasingly embattled entity."[10]

This is why "fake news," viral misinformation, and conspiracy theories are increasingly problems. Speed often leads to errors. It makes us susceptible to falling for false reports and passing along misinformation. And it's not just amateur bloggers and Facebook posters who are susceptible to this. Even society's most esteemed experts and hallowed institutions are vulnerable to the mistakes that come with commenting or reporting on something faster than it can be understood. If the *New York Times* can fall into the Internet speed trap of too-hasty and inaccurate reportage, who can be trusted? If the Centers for Disease Control doesn't provide reliable information on the dynamics of a contagion and how best to contain it, who does? Over time our skepticism about all sources leads us to turn inward, trusting only in ourselves—which brings us to our third major bad dietary habit.

3. EATING ONLY WHAT TASTES GOOD TO ME

If we only ever ate our favorite foods, most of us would be sick or dead. I love almond croissants and chocolate chip cookies (especially paired with a cup of black coffee!), but a diet consisting only of this would land me in the hospital. So it is with our information diet. We might be tempted to consume only material we like and have a taste for, but that will leave us sickly. Sadly, this is exactly what many of us do in today's hyper-individualistic, choose-your-own-adventure world.

The Internet is built around *you*. Google search; social media algorithms; recommendations from Siri, Alexa, Netflix, and Spotify; and even the creepy artificial intelligence that now finishes your sentences in email writing: all of it is tailored to *you*. In theory this is amazing! What's wrong with a world that revolves around *you* and your particular preferences and proclivities? A few things.

First, when everything revolves around you and your tastes, it's only going to be awesome if you know exactly what's good for you. And we usually don't. Consider the build-your-own pizza restaurant trend. You go down the line and pick exactly what you want on your pizza: the spicy marinara sauce, sausage, pepperoni, olives, red onions, garlic, ricotta, mozzarella, maybe some pesto drizzled on top. Whatever suits your fancy. But in my experience (and maybe I'm just a bad pizza maker), the "perfect pizza for me" almost always ends up being a disappointment. Generally I would have been better off simply trusting the expertise of the chef, allowing someone with actual culinary wisdom to create a pizza I'd be sure to enjoy. Furthermore, if it's always only up to me to build my own pizza, I'll likely only stick with flavors I know and like, never venturing into new culinary territory or expanding my palate.

The second problem is that when every individual is living a totally unique, customized, perfectly curated "i" life, it is harder to find commonality with others. We start losing the ability to be empathetic, unable to connect with people because their experience of the world—the news they consume, their social media feeds, and so on—is different from ours in ways we can't even know. We are all living in our own self-made media bubbles, and no two are the same. Part of the reason society is increasingly divisive is that we can't have productive conversations when everyone comes to it with their own set of "facts," "experts," and background biases, having been shaped by an information diet completely different from anyone else's. And when we can't relate to others, we retreat further into our individualistic, self-referential bubbles, which is not an environment where wisdom can grow.

A Healthier Diet

So what do we do about these bad dietary habits that are poisoning our souls? Shouldn't Christians, as followers of the man who called himself "the truth" (John 14:6) and said "the truth will set you free" (John 8:32), be leading the charge to recover truth and model wisdom in a post-truth age?

Some Christians have suggested the cultural situation is so dire, and the malforming momentum of the digital age so unstoppable, that the best strategy is to withdraw. In order to avoid infection by the contagions of the digital age, we should unplug and form alternative communities somewhere, like the monks in the Dark Ages. If we want to remain salt and light for future generations and be carriers of Christian wisdom beyond this troubling era, we need to hunker down and wait it out, lest we lose ourselves in the onslaught.

So the logic goes. And it makes some sense. In my more cynical moments, when I see the disturbing tendencies in my own knowledge-intake habits and fret about how my sons will fare in such a climate, I too am tempted to throw my phone down the garbage disposal and chuck my computer off the roof. I sometimes dream of building a L'Abri-style knowledge institution in some beautiful desert or mountain landscape, full of books and free of phones.

But then I remember that throughout Christian history, followers of Jesus haven't run *away* from the sick for fear of getting infected themselves; they've stayed *with* the sick and tried to help them. From the Christians who cared for their pagan neighbors suffering from the devastating plagues of the early Roman empire to medical missionaries Nancy Writebol and Dr. Kent Brantly (who in 2014 contracted Ebola while treating victims of the disease in West Africa[11]), followers of Jesus have done what Jesus did. Rather than avoiding the leper, the prostitute, the opioid addict, and the homeless schizophrenic, Christians have moved toward them. Rather than saving themselves in escape, they sacrificed their safety in service.

This is what we must do in this era of epistemological sickness. Yes, to stay in this toxic information environment is to risk becoming further infected by the ailments that already plague us. But to leave is to abandon the lost to an even darker lostness.

The world needs wisdom desperately, truth that is unshakable and foundations that are solid. Only Christianity provides this sort of wisdom, and it's exactly the medicine our ailing culture needs. In order to bring the light of Christian wisdom to the darkness of our unwise age, however, Christians must recover habits of wisdom in their own lives. We need a diet built around knowledge intake that actually cultivates wisdom. We need for our mental and spiritual health what the Food Pyramid was for our physical health: guidance for what to eat and what not to eat and in what proportions, so we can become more healthy and strong.

This is what *The Wisdom Pyramid* is about. It's a plan for stabilizing a sick society by making Christians wiser: God-fearing, trustworthy truth-tellers and truth-livers. Salt and light. This is what we are called to be. This is what the world desperately needs us to be.

DISCUSSION QUESTIONS

1. Why does it seem like there is an inverse correlation between information and wisdom ("Our world has more and more information, but less and less wisdom," p. 11)?

2. How have you personally felt mental and spiritual sickness in the digital age?

3. Of the three poor habits of informational "eating"—too much, too fast, too focused on me—which do you struggle with most?

Part One

SOURCES OF OUR SICKNESS

Chapter 1

INFORMATION GLUTTONY

Where is the wisdom we have lost in knowledge?
Where is the knowledge we have lost in
information? T.S. ELIOT, *THE ROCK*

THE EXPONENTIAL EXPLOSION OF information in the "information age" is mind-boggling. Consider a sampling of the numbers. In 2019, *a single minute* on the Internet saw the transmission of 188 million emails, 18.1 million texts, and 4.5 million videos viewed on YouTube.[1] By 2020, there were 40 times more bytes of data on the Internet than there are stars in the observable universe. Some estimates suggest that by 2025, 463 exabytes of data will be created each day online—the equivalent of 212,765,957 DVDs per day.[2] What even is an *exabyte*? Well, consider this: five exabytes is equivalent to all words ever spoken by humans since the dawn of time.[3] In 2025, that amount of data will be created every 15 minutes.

Here's the craziest thing: It's all in our pockets, just a few clicks away. Our phones are now encyclopedias. Libraries. Universities. Universes. But as convenient as it is to have such access—answers to any question we might have, results for any painting or video we want to see, ump-teen resources for whatever we might want to research—the glut of information online is also overwhelming. And it is not making us wise.

Just as too much food makes a body sick, too much information makes the soul sick. Information gluttony is a real problem in the age of Google—its symptoms are widespread and concerning. Here are five of them.

Symptom 1: Anxiety and Stress

Too much of anything causes problems for our health. This is as true of the information we take in as it is of the foods we consume. The information bombardment we increasingly face—characterized by nonstop swiping, scrolling, viewing, listening, reading, texting, and multitasking from morning to night—is creating stress in our brains and contributing to rising levels of anxiety. Our brains are shockingly adaptable and resilient, but they have limits.

Today's frenetic information landscape is making our brains busier than ever: the information triage that our over-burdened brains must constantly perform naturally drains huge amounts of energy. Con-stant multitasking also drains energy: making a dinner reservation on Yelp between replying to mom's text, sending a work email, and watching a "must-see" video a friend just shared on Facebook within the span of five minutes. This sort of extreme multitasking, notes neuroscientist Daniel Levitin, overstimulates and stresses our brains:

> Asking the brain to shift attention from one activity to another causes the prefrontal cortex and striatum to burn up oxygenated glucose, the same fuel they need to stay on task. And the kind of rapid, continual shifting we do with multitasking causes the brain to burn through fuel so quickly that we feel exhausted and disoriented

after even a short time. We've literally depleted the nutrients in our brain. This leads to compromises in both cognitive and physical performance. Among other things, repeated task switching leads to anxiety, which raises levels of the stress hormone cortisol in the brain, which in turn can lead to aggressive and impulsive behaviour.[4]

Another way the information glut causes stress and anxiety is that we burden ourselves with massive amounts of unnecessary and often troubling knowledge. When we are physically sick, we search WebMD to find answers and usually only find more to worry about. As if our own struggles and family complexities were not emotionally burdensome enough, our Instagram and Facebook feeds pull us into the pleas, rants, and emotional vortexes of hundreds of others throughout the day. The constant news notifications of Amber Alerts, deadly tornadoes, measles outbreaks, school shootings, "suspicious activity" in our neighborhoods (thanks to apps like NextDoor), and all manner of horrific crime headlines accumulate in our consciousness, burdening our brains with anxiety about the mounting number of ways the world can kill us. Our FitBits, diet apps, and other health gadgets provide information about our bodies that can be helpful in moderation but that can easily become an anxiety-fueling obsession.

It's not that information of this sort is always bad or unhelpful. It's just that the cumulative effect of too much information—so easily and constantly accessible to us—creates a burden that our minds and souls were not created to bear.

Symptom 2: Disorientation and Fragmentation

The information barrage comes at us each day in disconnected, undifferentiated, all-over-the-place ways. Our social media feeds—no respecters of logical flow or the need for synthesis—embody this. Open your Facebook, Twitter, or Instagram feed now, and you'll see this: a movie trailer next to an article about abortion; a photo from a friend's Texas road trip followed by someone else promoting their podcast.

It naturally leaves our heads spinning and—over time—our hearts battered and ultimately numb. It's obituaries next to baby announcements, cry-for-help laments next to "look at my best life!" vacation photos. Sports scores next to Augustine quotes. Worship music next to snake-chasing-iguana videos. John Piper sermons between sessions of Fortnite and Duolingo language learning. In the words of Arcade Fire, it's "Everything Now!"

In addition to causing cognitive dizziness, this indistinguishable array of information erodes our ability to distinguish between the trivial and the truly important. Over time we come to value information more for its spectacle—infotainment—than for the complex realities it signifies. Our news feeds are the amusement parks, penny arcades, and vaudeville stages of the digital era.

Media critic Neil Postman saw this coming in the 1980s, when he observed that televised news had become a sort of variety show of disconnected amusements meant to keep viewers tuned in:

> "Now . . . this" is commonly used on radio and television newscasts to indicate that what one has just heard or seen has no relevance to what one is about to hear or see, or possibly to anything one is ever likely to hear or see. The phrase is a means of acknowledging the fact that the world as mapped by the speeded-up electronic media has no order or meaning and is not to be taken seriously. There is no murder so brutal, no earthquake so devastating, no political blunder so costly—for that matter, no ball score so tantalizing or weather report so threatening—that it cannot be erased from our minds by a newscaster saying, "Now . . . this."[5]

In addition to these numbing and desensitizing effects, the constant hum of our information feeds fragments our lives. Instead of being present with our families, we are present with the hordes demanding our attention on email, text, Voxer, WhatsApp, Messenger, and umpteen other communication platforms. Instead of being present in the places where we live, we are present in the crises across the world and the trending debates on placeless Twitter. Our feeds bring the world and all its chaos into our minds, splitting our attention in a hundred different ways.

We weren't made for this. Writing a half century ago in *The Technological Society*, French Protestant theologian Jacques Ellul observed:

> [Man] was made to go six kilometers an hour, and he goes a thousand . . . He was made to have contact with living things, and he lives in a world of stone. He was created with a certain essential unity, and he is fragmented by all the forces of the modern world.[6]

Ironically, as much as the information age (and its "global village") promises to broaden our horizons and create healthy, integrated, well-informed global citizens, in reality it has had the opposite effect. The hyper-connection and over-awareness of a space-conquered world renders us fragmented and disconnected from *place*—the local contexts where we can know and be known and effect change to the greatest degree. As Ellul states, "The paradox is characteristic of our times, that to the abstract conquest of Space by Man (capitalized) corresponds the limitation of place for men (in small letters)."[7]

Symptom 3: Impotence

Our broader exposure to space, coupled with a diminished connection to *place*, leaves us feeling over-stimulated but under-activated. On any given day we are left inflamed by whatever grievances the Internet has exposed us to, yet we are impotent to do much, if anything, about it. The endless conveyor belt of content puts more things on our radar in a day than people a century ago would encounter in a year—often about places we've never heard of and issues we didn't know were issues.[8]

Postman talks about how our access to information and news from all over the world "gives us something to talk about but cannot lead to any meaningful action." This is the legacy of the telegraph, he says: "By generating an abundance of irrelevant information, it dramatically altered what may be called the information-action ratio."

Historically, Postman observes, information was deemed valuable insofar as it had the potential of leading to action. But the telegraph and later technologies rendered that relationship abstract and remote: "For the first time in human history, people were faced with the problem of information glut, which means that simultaneously they were faced with the problem of a diminished social and political potency."[9]

Social media epitomizes this. Our feeds constantly inform us of far-removed news about which we have very little context and even less recourse to action: political protests in Venezuela, volcanic eruption in New Zealand, a snake found in a toilet in Florida, and so on. We can easily come to the point where we spend hours attending to headlines about things that will never affect us, debates about things we know little about, and problems we cannot solve. Meanwhile, as we are consumed by the "far away" dramas of our social media spaces, we neglect the tangible realities of our immediate place—the local news, proximate debates, and immediate problems we could more meaningfully address.

After the telegraph, Postman argues, "Everything became everyone's business. For the first time, we were sent information which answered no question we had asked, and which, in any case, did not permit the right to reply."[10] Social media, of course, gives us permission to "reply"—but to what end? We may have a sense that our participation is meaningful action, that it is *doing something*, but more often than not we are only adding to the noise, getting needlessly angry, and contributing more irrelevant information to our already overloaded, exhausted brains.

Today's information landscape—which bombards us with grievances and trivialities we didn't go looking for but nevertheless get sucked into—dignifies irrelevance and amplifies importance, argues Postman. It all adds up to an inflated sense of the world's terribleness and an angst about our inability to do much about it.

Symptom 4: Decision and Commitment Paralysis

Another symptom of the sickness of information gluttony is a debilitating overabundance of choices. With literally everything at your digital disposal, how do you choose? Maybe you've experienced "Netflix Paralysis"—that moment when you're trying to decide what to watch, but you freeze because there are too many options and no external guidance for your selection. You're worried about wasting time, and the "will it be the perfect choice?" burden weighs heavily.[11]

When everything is at our disposal and to our liking, we'll naturally experience stress under the weight of FOMO (fear of missing out). Will we make the wrong choice? Of the fifteen shows your friends have talked about on social media, which one should you watch? These questions can be debilitating, adding to the anxiety that comes from what Alvin Toffler coined as "overchoice," in his 1970 book *Future Shock*.[12]

Overchoice in the world of streaming video is no joke. The amount of new content being released every month on YouTube, Facebook, Hulu, HBO, Disney+, Netflix, Amazon Prime, and all the rest, is mind-boggling. And as we become ever less able to make choices amid this overwhelming array of options, "suggested for you" algorithms will be ever-more adept at doing the work for us, eagerly serving up tailored "watch this next!" content that keeps us on the platform. Indeed, the stress of having to actively sift through viewing options tends to make us more passive, with little capacity for what Tony Reinke calls "spectacle resistance": "Our lazy eyes and incurious gaze are happily fed by the spectacle makers. We no longer seek out new spectacles; new spectacles seek us out."[13]

The effects of overchoice also pose problems beyond digital information. Wherever there is an abundance of options, we can struggle with commitment to anything. I see this often with church, for example. With a church "option" out there for every taste, preference, political leaning, and aesthetic (not to mention the option to just not go to church), the Christ-follower is positioned as a consumer whose attachment to a church is only as strong as a shopper's attached to a brand. When our tastes change, so do our commitments. Just as on Netflix we might only make it through two episodes of a series, or 20 minutes of a movie, before we lose interest and switch to something else, so do we approach church and spirituality as a fluid thing that should adapt to our shifting needs and moods.

Philosopher Charles Taylor calls this abundance of spiritual choice "the nova effect"—an "ever-widening variety of moral/spiritual options"[14]—and it figures prominently in his account of secularity in his monumental work, *A Secular Age*. Riffing on Taylor, Alan Noble observes that "decision overload is as much a problem for spirituality as it is for digital multitasking . . . A distracted and secular age does this to us: we are cognitively overwhelmed by the expanding horizon of possible beliefs."[15]

We are so overwhelmed with possible paths, possible sources of truth and theories of the good life, that we don't pick any path. Or we switch paths every few months. Or we cobble together our own just-for-me spiritual path, pulling bits and pieces of theology, philosophy, morality, and aesthetics from all manner of disconnected sources. Because we can.

Symptom 5: Confirmation Bias

Because there is limitless space online, every conspiracy theory, every quirky niche, and every cult-like community has a space to flourish. Whatever you believe, or whatever you might be tempted to believe, there is information online to back you up. And it's not just the dark web we're talking about here, where trolls and terrorists find reinforcement for their extremist beliefs. We're all susceptible to the path of least cognitive resistance: selecting sources that harmonize with our existing beliefs and don't complicate our paradigms or rile us up.

Who can blame us? It's why Americans traveling in a foreign country might opt to buy coffee in a Starbucks rather than at one of the (probably much better) local cafes. In noisy and cognitively overwhelming spaces, there is comfort in known commodities. Maryanne Wolf puts it this way:

> We need to confront the reality that when bombarded with too many options, our default can be to rely on information that places few demands upon thinking. More and more of us would then think we know something based on information whose source was chosen because it conforms to how and what we thought before.[16]

In a world of increasing overchoice, this is an increasingly dangerous, if understandable, coping mechanism. We triage our personal information chaos by cultivating feeds full of voices of comfort rather than voices that make our blood boil. Who has time or mental space for that? Unfollow.

Recognizing the twenty-first-century person's struggle to sift through the information glut and incentivized to make their platforms pleasant and not toxic spaces, social media companies make the confirmation bias problem worse through personalized algorithms. The result is unique-to-every-user feeds that create a world where no two people see the same information. We all live on islands of algorithm-fueled fantasy and confirmation bias. It's no wonder tribalism is on the rise. It's no wonder everyone is talking past each other.

Computer scientist Jaron Lanier, author of *Ten Arguments for Deleting Your Social Media Accounts Right Now*, calls this algorithm-fueled fragmentation an "epochal development" that is making it harder to understand and empathize with each other.

> The version of the world you are seeing is invisible to the people who misunderstand you, and vice versa . . . We see less than ever before of what others are seeing, so we have less opportunity to understand each other.[17]

The Devil Delights

It's easy to imagine the devil delighting in all this: angry tribalism, addictive triviality, amusing ourselves to death. As humans become more stressed, numbed, disoriented, distracted, and paralyzed by the impenetrable glut of information, chaos reigns. As chaos reigns, sin thrives.

It's interesting that the fall of man in Genesis 3 came about because of temptations of *knowledge*: fruit from the tree of the knowledge of good and evil. In our age too, the lure of infinite, godlike knowledge wreaks havoc. I sometimes ponder that the logo on my iPhone—

a device that approximates godlike knowledge if ever there was one—
is an apple with a bite mark. A nod to Eve's original sin? An ode to
humanity's insatiable hunger for infinite knowledge? Perhaps.[18] But
just as for Adam and Eve in Eden, so it is for us: the desire to know
everything only leads to grief.

DISCUSSION QUESTIONS

1. Which of the "symptoms" of information overload discussed in this
chapter do you experience the most?

2. What are some areas where you feel like access to too much information has been a burden or done more harm than good?

3. Why is it important to have a connection between information
and action? Think of examples in your own life of where there is a
connection between information and action, and where there isn't a
connection.

Chapter 2

PERPETUAL NOVELTY

Now just as we pick out and exaggerate the pleasure of eating
to produce gluttony, so we pick out this natural pleasantness
of change and twist it into a demand for absolute novelty.
SCREWTAPE (IN C. S. LEWIS'S *THE SCREWTAPE LETTERS*)

CAN YOU NAME FIVE news events that happened last week? What about four people you texted yesterday? Or three things you watched on TV or a streaming site today? If you're like me, you struggle to recall the information and entertainment (or infotainment) you encountered in the last week, let alone in the last hour. This is because the overwhelming *amount* of content entering our brains today is also coming at an overwhelming *pace*.

Internet speeds are getting faster every year. In 2018, broadband download speeds in the U.S. rose 35.8 percent over 2017.[1] Across the world, the global average for mobile download speed increased 15.2 percent over 2017.[2] Speed is paramount in the attention economy, as content providers want to keep consumers on their platforms without losing them due to any lag time. The speedier-than-ever information flow may be a boon for the state of digital business, but it's a bust for the state of human wisdom.

Just as eating *too much* food makes us sick, eating *too fast* also makes us ill. Scarfing down food quickly may satiate our immediate hunger or need for "on the go" fuel, but it usually isn't great for our health. Similar things happen when we consume information too fast. It may seem like we are maximizing time and optimizing ourselves—efficiently consuming all manner of information at ever greater speeds—but the reality is we are eroding our capacity for wisdom.

The Horror of the Same Old Thing

Humans have always been fidgety creatures. The Internet and other technologies may be exacerbating this tendency, but they did not create it. Adam and Eve's fidgety fingers couldn't help themselves in Eden, and ever since humans have struggled with contentment: we want more than what we have, and we want it now.

The devil delights in this tendency and preys on it. In *The Screwtape Letters*, C. S. Lewis brilliantly captures how vulnerable we are because of our aversion to "the horror of the Same Old Thing." Screwtape (an experienced demon) advises his nephew Wormwood (a demon in training) to exploit the human demand for novelty: "This demand is valuable in various ways. In the first place it diminishes pleasure while increasing desire. The pleasure of novelty is by its very nature more subject than any other to the law of diminishing returns."[3]

Never has the devil's work been easier in the area of novelty obsession. We check our smartphones upwards of two hundred times per day, filling every open space in life with whatever new things can be scrolled through: in line at Target, in our car at stop lights, at the dinner table, on the toilet. Our phone is usually the first thing we look at in the morning and the last thing we look at before bed.

Instead of being content with silence in the "in between" moments of life, our fidgety fingers can't help but reach for the phone—so we can do something, *anything*, to maximize the time. Indeed, the podcast craze coincides with the mobile-fueled frenzy to "redeem every moment" by listening to episodes while we clean the house or commute to work, or perhaps we listen to an audiobook while we go for a jog.

There's no shortage of content clamoring for our attention—much of it is *good* content—and the pressure to "watch this, read that, listen to this!" can be hard to resist. But what is all this doing to our brains?

The research is not encouraging.

Our Changing Brains

In *The Shallows*, Nicholas Carr calls the Internet "a technology of forgetfulness" and describes how, thanks to the plasticity of our neural pathways, our brains are literally being rewired by digital distraction:

> The more we use the Web, the more we train our brain to be distracted—to process information very quickly and very efficiently but without sustained attention. That helps explain why many of us find it hard to concentrate even when we're away from our computers. Our brains become adept at forgetting, inept at remembering.[4]

Though we are reading a *ton* on our devices and screens—we actually read a novel's worth of words every day—it is not the sort of continuous, sustained, concentrated reading conducive to reflective thinking. Maryanne Wolf argues: "There is neither the time nor the impetus for the nurturing of a quiet eye, much less the memory of its harvests."[5]

Our rapid-fire toggling between spectacles—an episode of a Hulu show here, a Spotify album there—works against wisdom in the *moment*, by eliminating any time for reflection or synthesis before the next thing beckons. But it also works against wisdom in the *long term*, as brain research is showing. Our overstimulated brains are becoming weaker, less critical, and more gullible at a time in history when we need them to be sharper than ever.

Quick Answers Instead of Slow Reflection

Google offers quick answers to any query we might have. But wisdom is not about getting to answers as fast as possible. It's more often about the journey, the bigger picture, the questions and complications along the way. Google's speedy delivery of answers is efficient, but it's not as nutritious or enjoyable for our souls. It's like treating food only as fuel and forsaking the value of slowly making and enjoying a meal.

The speed and access of information has conditioned us to gather information impatiently. Skimming has become the default way people read. In this world, notes Carr, "We are evolving from being cultivators of personal knowledge to being hunters and gatherers in the electronic data forest. . . . The strip-mining of 'relevant content' replaces the slow excavation of meaning."[6] This has consequences for the brain, which may become more skillful at the strip-mining approach to fast-food information, but loses the ability to slowly stew over things that require synthesis and introspection. We move quickly from thing to thing but fail to see how the things connect. We can gather information faster than ever, but we are losing the ability to process it in a way that fully absorbs its nutrients.

Perceptual Presentism

Compounding the problem is what I call "perceptual presentism," where reality is filtered to us in fleeting fragments of *what's happening now*, rather than through the filter of time and generational wisdom. Real-time tweets and Facebook posts that often discuss whatever the day's trending debate is now dominate our attention. Status updates and disappear-in-a-day stories populate our perceptual field. It's called *Insta*gram for a reason, after all. Timeliness becomes an addictive toxin. Immediacy becomes an idol.

But this approach to time is not only narcissistic; it's dangerous. It disconnects us from the wisdom of history and places undue mental emphasis on (and blind trust in) that which is least likely to produce wisdom: the untested *now*. C. S. Lewis called this emphasis on now "chronological snobbery," defined as "the uncritical acceptance of the intellectual climate common to our own age and the assumption that whatever has gone out of date is on that account discredited."[7] Catholic philosopher Augusto Del Noce, writing in 1970, put it this way: "Today's man, cut off from the past and from the future, lives through a sequence of discontinuous instants. . . . Perfect novelty is his oxygen."[8]

In a sobering 2019 *Atlantic* article, Jonathan Haidt and Tobias Rose-Stockwell note the problematic way that ideas and conflicts of the present moment "dominate and displace older ideas and the lessons of the past." One paradox of the information age, they observe, is that even as younger generations grow up with unprecedented access to everything that has ever been written and digitized, the new generations nevertheless "find themselves less familiar with the accumulated wisdom of humanity than any recent generation, and therefore [are] more prone to embrace ideas that bring social prestige within their immediate network [and] yet are ultimately misguided."[9]

Today's technological landscape hasn't invented this sort of problematic presentism, but it has amplified it. Our existing human inclinations toward the latest and the trendiest are accelerated by the breakneck speed with which things come and go. This presentist orientation is particularly toxic (and all too common) in evangelical faith communities, where obsessions with "relevance," an uncritical embrace of technology, and a disconnection from history leave many churches vulnerable to being molded more by the ephemeral spirit of the age than by the solid, time-tested wisdom of ages past.

Presentism is toxic not only because it rejects the resources of the past, but also because it has little discipline to stay on course for the future. Orientation around the new is by definition unstable, because the "new" quickly becomes "old" and passé. The presentist world burns through fads and ideas at an alarming pace. Among other things, this undermines the sorts of qualities—grit, perseverance, long-haul commitment—that are essential to actually solving complex problems. Presentism leads us to be "all in" for some cause for a few months, only to lose interest when another cause grabs our attention. It turns us into fickle consumer "slacktivists" whose short bursts of passion—for a new weight loss scheme, a buzzy Netflix show, a hashtag campaign against some injustice—move the needle on nothing except the profit margin for the platforms that benefit from our now-ness.

The Business of Our Attention

Our novelty obsession fuels consumerism. Our restless desire for the "new" (clothes, cars, gadgets, artisan coffee, etc.) keeps countless industries afloat. Our constant demand for new spectacles and new controversies has made Silicon Valley CEOs billionaires. It's in the best interest of tech titans to keep us constantly fed with what Tony Reinke calls "microspectacles"—viral video clips, controversial tweets, memes, and "attention candy" that feed our appetite "for something new, weird, glorious, hilarious, curious, or cute."[10] These media companies know candy can be addictive (even if we know it's terrible for us), and they want us hooked. They've become experts at packaging stimuli in ways our brains find irresistible, argues Matthew Crawford, "just as food engineers have become expert in creating 'hyperpalatable' foods by manipulating levels of sugar, fat, and salt." Our subsequent distractibility, thus, "might be regarded as the mental equivalent of obesity."[11]

Facebook cofounder Sean Parker admitted, in an infamous 2017 interview, that the thought process behind Facebook was, "How do we consume as much of your time and conscious attention as possible? And that means that we needed to sort of give you a little dopamine hit every once in a while because someone liked or commented on a photo or a post or whatever."[12] This is why the dings and push-notifications that bombard us hourly are so effective. They give us a dopamine rush, similar to what keeps gamblers addicted to slot machines: we unconsciously click and—*poof!*—we're back on the platform without knowing why, our attention steered toward yet another microspectacle. As Carr notes, "It's in Google's economic interest to make sure we click as often as possible. The last thing the company wants is to encourage leisurely reading or slow, concentrated thought. Google is, quite literally, in the business of distraction."[13]

But it's not just Google and Facebook who are fighting for the lucrative commodity of our attention. It's every content producer. With more and more competition for eyeballs that have shorter and shorter attention spans, all media publishers must resort to desperate measures to win our coveted clicks. This is one reason journalism has seen better days. In today's microspectacle world, what wins in the attention game is often the hot take, the incendiary headline, the rashly reported story, the "breaking news" that isn't actually newsworthy. Cable news channels have far more air time to fill than there is real news to report, so they stack their schedules with talking head commentary, partisan debates, salacious scandals, celebrity divorces, and other infotainment to keep viewers glued to their screens—at least until another "breaking news" alert or "must see" viral video draws the viewer's attention elsewhere.

Vulnerability to Fake News

The speed of the news cycle and our decreasing capacity for slow, careful thinking is having another troubling effect: we are increasingly gullible and complicit in the spread of fake news. Just as reporters increasingly rush to break "news" first, so we are often in a rush to opine or rage about the latest headlines. In both cases, speed works against accuracy and prudence.

The rise of #FakeNews is not just about Russian bots and nefarious political propaganda. It's something even prestigious news outlets struggle with. Consider the case of Jussie Smollett. In January 2019, the *Empire* actor—who is gay and black—told Chicago police he was attacked by two men who put a rope around his neck while shouting racist and homophobic epithets. Almost every major news outlet made much of the story, which was fodder for the popular narrative about a rise of brazen hate crimes in Trump's America. One *Daily Beast* reporter tweeted that the attack proved support from Trump was "tantamount to providing artillery for weaponized bigotry."[14] Except later it turned out that Smollett staged the attack for publicity. The speed of reporting and the speed of the social media rage cycle propelled the story virally, just as Smollett had wanted. Everyone was duped.

Good reporting takes time. Sources must be verified. The fuller picture of out-of-context quotes, images, and videos must be sought. But the "fortune favors the fast" nature of journalism today often skips these essential steps. Further, we consumers are often eager to share things on the spot. Our quick-draw posture on social media is often "post first, think later" (if we think at all). This is disastrous—not only because it makes us easy to manipulate, but also because it erodes our credibility and can do great harm to others.

The temptation in today's world is to make every thought public. But is this wise? Some of the wisest people I know are very slow to publicly share their opinions. They recognize the fallibility of first impressions and the folly of "*insta*-reaction." Kevin DeYoung noted recently that one of the distinguishing marks of a "quarrelsome person" is that he or she has no unarticulated opinions. "Do people know what you think of everything?" DeYoung asks. "They shouldn't. That's why you have a journal or a prayer closet or a dog."[15]

One of the most valuable areas of biblical wisdom we need for our day is the taming of the tongue. Before we sound off online, we should remember proverbs like:

- "Whoever guards his mouth preserves his life; he who opens wide his lips comes to ruin" (Prov. 13:3).
- "Whoever is slow to anger has great understanding, but he who has a hasty temper exalts folly" (Prov. 14:29).
- "Whoever keeps his mouth and his tongue keeps himself out of trouble" (Prov. 21:23).

Or there is James 1:19—a verse that, if heeded, would prevent all manner of grief in today's world (but would also probably put social media out of business): "Let every person be quick to hear, slow to speak, slow to anger." The problem, of course, is that today's media economy is fueled by "quick to speak" rants, mobs, and pile-ons that create traffic spikes and trending topics. To resist this temptation is one of the most challenging yet subversive things a wisdom-seeking Christian can do.

"The real strength of the good soldier of Jesus Christ," wrote Jonathan Edwards nearly three hundred years ago,

> is simply the steadfast maintenance of a holy calmness . . . sustained amidst all the storms, injuries, wrong behavior, and unexpected acts and events in this evil and unreasonable world. The Scripture seems to intimate that true fortitude consists chiefly of this: "He that is slow to anger, is better than the mighty; and he that rules his spirit, than he that takes a city" (Proverbs 16:32).[16]

The Folly of Distractibility

In Proverbs, the opposite of wisdom is often personified in a character known as "the forbidden woman." A woman of "smooth words" (Prov. 2:16–17) whose lips "drip honey" (5:3), she is "loud," "seductive," and "sits at the door of her house," "calling to those who pass by" (9:13–15). A. W. Tozer describes her as "moral folly personified" who "works by the power of suggestion." In today's world, we see the "forbidden woman" at work through "watch this next!" algorithms that lure us into constant distraction by putting "suggestions" into our minds. Here's Tozer:

> Many are brainwashed from nine o'clock in the morning or earlier until the last eyelid flutters shut at night because of the power of suggestion. These people are uncommitted. They go through life uncommitted, not sure in which direction they are going.[17]

Here we see the crux of why today's media environment is so prone to leading us into folly. When we pick up our phones aimlessly, scroll our feeds without a goal in mind, or suggest to our spouse that "we should watch something on Netflix," we are uncommitted. We are vulnerable to the power of suggestion, cogs in the machinery of algorithms ever more sophisticated at keeping us distracted on their platforms. We are digital *wanderers*, and this is a dangerous thing to be.

The antidote to dangerous distractibility is purpose, focus, and intention. Proverbs 4:25 says, "Let your eyes look directly forward, and your gaze be straight before you." This is wisdom in contrast to the unwise woman of folly, who "does not ponder the path of life; her ways wander, and she does not know it" (Prov. 5:6).

When you go online, ask yourself what you are going online to do. Is there a specific goal? When you open YouTube, is it to watch a specific thing? When you reach for your phone as you wait in line or walk from one place to another, is it for a purpose or just out of habit? When we aren't going *somewhere*, we'll go anywhere—and the "anywheres" of the Internet are rarely good for us.

DISCUSSION QUESTIONS

1. In what practical ways can Christians model a slower, wiser pace in a sped-up world?

2. Discuss specific, recent examples of how the speed of news reporting and dissemination has worked against truth. What can we do to guard against the spreading of "fake" or haphazardly reported news?

3. Why is being a "digital wanderer" so dangerous? What practical steps can we take to guard against aimless scrolling and clicking online?

Chapter 3

"LOOK WITHIN" AUTONOMY

It was precisely because man welcomed the prospect
of becoming the measure and judge of all things
that sin first entered the world. J. I. PACKER

ONE OF THE BY-PRODUCTS of information's glut and speed is that
we are increasingly skeptical about its trustworthiness. There is so
much *bad* information out there, so much that is false and fake and
corrupted by bias. It's no wonder we increasingly cope by seeing ourselves as the most trustworthy source. It's no wonder "look within,"
"follow your heart," and "you do you" are resonant phrases. External
authorities like family, teachers, pastors, politicians, religious traditions, and others have disappointed us or been proven hypocritical. At
best we see them as secondary to the self as sources of truth. At worst
we dismiss them as oppressive obstacles on the path to self-discovery.

But the self is not the reliable authority it is cracked up to be. Our
fickle hearts are unreliable guides, deceitful above all things (Jer. 17:9).
Our embrace of "being true to ourselves" often leads to a closed loop
of self-deception and chronic brokenness, where we erroneously

believe we have all the resources for healing within ourselves. We buy into the notion that we exist as isolated, self-contained creatures who needn't be accountable to anything beyond ourselves. But this is a dangerous and lonely lie.

Just as it's dangerous to eat *too much* food and to eat food *too fast*, so is it unhealthy to eat food that is *untested*—food *you* deem edible or nutritious based only on *your* personal tastes, preferences, or gut instincts. Imagine if you're in the forest and you pick a mushroom or a berry to eat just because you think it *looks* edible. In this case, self-appointed expertise could literally kill you. There's a reason nutrition labels exist. Without any regulation or guardrails beyond the "gut instincts" of our consumer hankerings, food might be dangerous.

So it is with knowledge, truth, and wisdom.

The Death of Expertise

The "look within" tendency to shun authority is as old as Eden. It was refined by Enlightenment thinkers like René Descartes and John Locke, who located truth in the individual's mental world, not in the world outside our heads. But the last century has seen an acceleration in the erosion of external authority.

The Internet's democratization of information has had a leveling effect that tends to downplay credentials and embolden unqualified participation in every area of discourse. We are now all "experts" on everything and have platforms to publish our thoughts. Actresses can launch lifestyle blogs that proffer all manner of dubious health advice. Some suburban moms declare themselves experts on vaccines, essential oils, alternative medicine, and special diets after reading a few blog posts (written by nonprofessional "experts"). Instagram influencers can confidently share opinions on political hot topics they know little to nothing about. During the COVID-19 pandemic, everyone with a Twitter account became strangely confident in their grasp of epidemiology and virus containment strategies.

"Expertise" has fallen on hard times. Often driven by class antagonism and resentment toward "elites," dismissal of credential-based authority is widespread and troubling. Tom Nichols published an excellent book about this in 2017, *The Death of Expertise*, in which he observes how this phenomenon wrongly construes the equal rights of "democracy" as also meaning equal talents, equal abilities, and equal knowledge.[1] It's a world where one man's opinion about something is as valid as the next guy's, even if the first man only heard something on talk radio about the subject while the "next guy" has a PhD in the subject.

As COVID-19 vividly demonstrated, "experts" are certainly not infallible, and blind trust in groupthink-susceptible classes of specialized scholars and bureaucrats can be a dangerous thing. Deep knowledge about a subject is no substitute for wisdom. Horrific wars, genocidal plots, and nefarious scientific enterprises have been perpetrated by experts with PhDs and esteemed credentials. But accumulated knowledge should count for *something*, shouldn't it? When enough members of a society dismiss established expertise in favor of their own proofless opinions and gut instincts, bad things happen. Left to our own inclinations, chaos often reigns. Just read the book of Judges, where "everyone did what was right in his own eyes" (Judg. 17:6).

Experts are usually *not* out to get us. They want to help us. Guardrails and gatekeepers are not about stifling us. They're about protecting us. Authority can be abused, yes, but at its best it is for our good. Writers are better off with editors. Children are better off with parents. Faced with a daunting restaurant menu full of tasty sounding options, we're better off asking the waiter for recommendations.

When we shun the advice of experts, we not only risk being exposed to bad things; we also miss out on good things. I'm a movie critic, which is one of those jobs that feels especially vulnerable in the "death of expertise" era. People assume because they also watch movies they are just as qualified as professional critics to evaluate film. But I've devoted fifteen years of my life to writing critically about movies. I earned a master's degree in cinema and media studies. I'm not offended when people reject or devalue my writing about film, I'm just disappointed. My goal in writing critical reviews is not about me wielding my expertise on film in an elitist way; I'm doing this to *help* people find the best films and avoid the bad ones. I don't want my critical expertise to *replace* the critical engagement of everyday moviegoers, but to enhance it.

We can't all be experts in everything. God gifts people differently for a reason. The biblical vision of a healthy church, for example, is not one where everyone contributes in the *same* way, but where variously gifted parts contribute to a healthier whole (see 1 Cor. 12:12–28; Eph. 4:1–16 among others). We need each other because we can't do everything on our own. We need to be educated and apprenticed by *others* if we are to become truly knowledgeable or skillful in any area. Rather than resenting the expertise of others, we should respect it and learn from it.

"Alternative Facts"

"Alternative facts" famously entered the cultural lexicon in early 2017 when Kellyanne Conway told Chuck Todd on *Meet the Press* (in reference to the disputed crowd size at Trump's inauguration), "You're saying it's a falsehood, and [we are] giving alternative facts to that." To which Todd went on to reply: "Alternative facts are not facts—they're falsehoods."[2]

In today's post-truth world, "facts" are seen as fluid, bias-laden things to dispute or ignore when they threaten us. Political debates are largely unproductive in part because both sides marshal their own sets of "facts" and simply dismiss the other side's arguments as invalid. Feelings now overrule facts. We assert as facts what we *feel* to be true, and when someone challenges us, we turn it back on them, because how dare they question the validity of our feelings? To have one's *felt* truth invalidated is to have one's very identity dismissed. It is to be offended, triggered, and "disrespected"—which is seen as more egregious than simply being proven wrong. However logical an argument might be, however indisputable the facts, it can all be dismissed as the "blindness" of privilege, the manipulation of the hegemony, or the weapon of the oppressor. Facts and rationality simply become inflictors of "trauma" (an increasingly weaponized word); not objective evidence in any agreed upon sense. "In a post-truth age," writes Abdu Murray, "if the evidence fits our preferences and opinions, then all is well and good. If it doesn't, then the evidence is deemed inadmissible or offensive, with offense being a kind of solvent against otherwise sound arguments."[3]

The same cavalier attitude toward facts also goes for our personal belief systems. In part because of the chaotic, incoherent flow of information that constantly fills our minds and also because our capacity for self-awareness and critical thinking is decreasing, we increasingly curate hodgepodge worldviews full of inherent contradictions. A person might adopt some aspects of Christianity but also some of Buddhism or Wicca, ignoring the fact that Christ claimed religious exclusivity (see John 14:6). Some might passionately support the protection of iguana eggs while advocating the legal killing of unborn human babies. Others might enthusiastically argue for the importance of organic crops and against the dangers of genetically modified tomatoes, even as they cheer the sex change operations and hormone modification of transgender persons. We increasingly fail to consider our own logical inconsistencies.

But because it's easy to just turn the channel or unfollow someone when our incoherent positions are challenged, we find it easy to keep holding contradictory views without feeling cognitive dissonance. "When confronted with a deficiency in our ethical code, it takes no real effort to ignore it," Alan Noble observes. In a world of constant mental stimulation, "our default response to cognitive dissonance is to simply do something else."[4]

All of this might sound crazy, and indeed it is. But it's how we live now. "Reality" isn't a force to reckon with as it once was. Established knowledge, provable facts, even the reality of one's own body—all of it can now be dismissed if it subverts the authority that matters most: the "self."

"Me" vs. My Body

A major source of confusion today stems from a body/person dualistic split, in which one's body is treated as separate (and less important) than one's person, which is the higher and more authentic "me." As Nancy Pearcey writes in *Love Thy Body*, this dualism often sets the body and person *against* each other, and as a result "demeans the body as extrinsic to the person—something inferior that can be used for purely pragmatic purposes."[5]

A utilitarian, dualistic view of the body leads us to obsess about optimizing its "performance" (exercise, dieting, nutrition supplements, protein bars, performance-enhancing drugs and surgeries, etc.), in a manner "akin to a luxury car owner polishing and tuning up an expensive automobile."[6] It also contributes to viewing sex as merely a physical act—a "pressure release valve" of our bodies (to extend the car metaphor). The rise of hookup culture, Tinder, and online pornography are part of this. The dualistic view also results in disturbing justifications for things like abortion and euthanasia. If "personhood" or the "real self" is not fundamentally connected to the physical body, it can be easy to claim that *mere bodies* (e.g., fetuses or people on feeding tubes) are not "persons" in any sense worth fighting for.

But perhaps the most flagrant example of body/person dualism is the rise of the LGBTQ movement and the larger division of "sex" and "gender" into two separate categories that have little (if anything) to do with biology. Gender theory today says your identity is what you feel, not what your biology suggests. Now the only standard for identity is one's assertion: "I identify as . . ." In a widely circulated YouTube video a few years ago, University of Washington students struggled to deny a 5'9" white man's assertion that he was a 6'5" Chinese woman.[7] How could they? If rationality and objectivity have given way to identity politics and "alternative facts," to deny someone's assertion of identity—however illogical it may be—is hateful and abusive; it is to deny their freedom to be a self-made "person."

But this brave new world is not freeing. Nor is it conducive to wisdom. Even as we empathize with those who truly do experience gender dysphoria (feeling psychologically or emotionally opposite from your biological sex), we must recognize that unhitching "gender identity" from bodily reality is not only a Pandora's box of subjectivism, but it's a sad diminishing of the physical. To sever the connection between the physical and the mental is really just a new form of gnosticism—a brazen denial of the goodness of God's creation and the intended harmony and interconnectedness between body and mind/soul.

Rejecting the Body's Truth

It is not a coincidence that the growing acceptance of a "gender identity" untethered to biology coincides with a technological society that is ever more ethereal and disembodied. As we increasingly live our lives through screens and keyboards, existing in the world of non-physical *representation* rather than physical, hand-to-the-plow *reality*, are we surprised it has become easier to grow detached from our bodies? Is it any wonder that we can begin to construct ourselves in ways that have no necessary connection to our bodies? It is perhaps unsurprising that the Wachowski brothers—the filmmaking duo whose *Matrix* franchise epitomized the "what is real" confusion of the digital age—are now the Wachowski *sisters*, having both transitioned into trans women.

This sort of digital gnosticism deceives us into thinking we are limitless because we supposedly aren't tied to our bodies. It makes possible such fields as "transhumanism"—the notion that technology will eventually enable humans to fully overcome the limitations of the body. Coupled with a centuries-long philosophical trajectory that has gradually liberated the "self" from the confines of all external authorities, the digital age now makes it acceptable to, among other things, "identify" as a woman even if you are biologically male.

In pre-digital, agrarian societies, such ideas would have never been *considered*. When you work with your hands as a craftsman, or toil in the fields from dusk till dawn, recognizing your body's capabilities and limitations is unavoidable. When you're a farmer you are more aware of the need for the body to rest, the need to clothe the body appropriately for weather, and the body's strength and fragility. This is partly why you find transgender people more often in cities and industrialized societies today than in rural or agrarian contexts. Disconnection from the realities of the physical world makes it easier to ignore the physical body in the conception of self.

But to reject the truth of the body, and more broadly of nature, is unwise. It leads to confusion and grief. When the only criterion for understanding something like gender (to use one example) is *whatever an individual* person says it is (e.g., "I am a woman because I feel that I am"), the very idea of "gender" becomes utterly meaningless. Language and agreed-upon definitions fall apart, and having coherent discourse about anything becomes increasingly difficult.

The Depressing Dead End of "Your Truth"

In her lifetime achievement award acceptance speech at the 2018 Golden Globes, Oprah Winfrey said, "What I know for sure is that speaking your truth is the most powerful tool we all have."[8]

Your truth. Those two words are so entrenched in our lexicon today that we hardly recognize them for the incoherent nightmare that they are. Among other things, the philosophy of "your truth" destroys families when a dad suddenly decides "his truth" is calling him to a new lover, a new family, or maybe even a new gender. It's a philosophy that can destroy entire societies, because invariably one person's truth will go to battle with another person's truth, and devoid of reason, only power decides the victor.

"Your truth" also puts an incredible, self-justifying burden on the individual. If we are all self-made projects whose destinies are wholly ours to discover and implement, life becomes a rat race of performative individuality. "Live your truth" autonomy is thus as exhausting as it is incoherent. As French sociologist Alain Ehrenberg points out in *The Weariness of the Self,* the self-creating person turns out to be fragile and "weary of her sovereignty." Depression is the inevitable result and "the inexorable counterpart of the human being who is her/his own sovereign."[9]

"Your truth" autonomy invariably leads to loneliness. It erroneously suggests we can live unencumbered and uninfluenced by the various structures that surround us (families, churches, cultures, biology, etc.). But it becomes impossible to form community when everyone is their own island, with no necessary reliance upon larger truths or embeddedness within a bigger story.

Again, these ideas were unfathomable in former eras, when to "go it alone" in life was seriously dangerous. In agrarian cultures the power of the communal is essential. Everyone plays a vital, interdependent role on the farm. You need each other to survive. Each person's identity is naturally understood in terms of how it relates to the whole. The idea of total autonomy is not only foolish and foreign; it's deadly.

In his excellent book, *The World Beyond Your Head*, Matthew B. Crawford challenges the idea that everything outside one's head is a potential threat to the self. His thesis is that the environments we exist within *constitute* rather than *compromise* the self. Humans are not just brains in vats. We are *situated* in real worlds we didn't make up, and we know ourselves not through abstract projections or self-conceptions, but in our "situatedness": "We live in a world that has already been named by our predecessors, and was saturated with meaning before we arrived."[10]

From cradle to grave, we are formed by others. Contrary to what a "look within" world would suggest, the world *outside* our heads defines our existence in ways we are foolish to ignore. Rather than seeing this as oppressive, or simply pretending (foolishly) this isn't the case, we should accept this situation as a gift: truth comes, in large part, from outside ourselves. We can choose the *sources* of where we look for truth. We can choose how we *synthesize* truth and *apply* it as wisdom in everyday circumstances. But we don't get to choose whether or not something is true. We don't *invent* truth. We don't determine it. We search it out and accept it with gratitude, even when it's at odds with our feelings or preferences.

Thanks be to God.

DISCUSSION QUESTIONS

1. Where have you seen the "death of expertise" at work in your community or more broadly in your culture? Why is self-appointed expertise so common today, and why is it problematic?

2. Phrases like "your truth," "follow your heart," and "be true to yourself" are so common today that to challenge them can come across as hateful. How would you lovingly challenge these ideas—and the preeminent authority of the self—in a conversation with a friend who espouses them?

3. Where have Christians and churches been complicit in perpetuating individualism and the erroneous (but common) notion of the autonomous self? How can we make accountability within a community appealing in an age of "you do you"?

Part Two

SOURCES OF OUR WISDOM

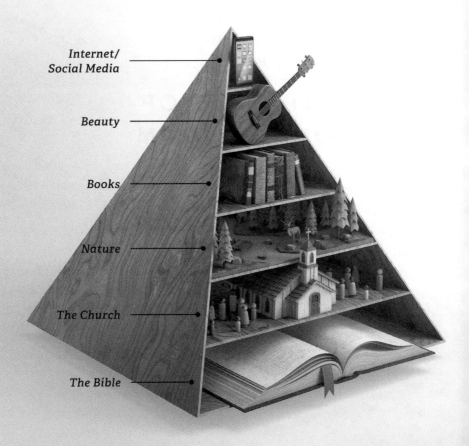

Internet/
Social Media

Beauty

Books

Nature

The Church

The Bible

Part Two Introduction

SOURCES OF TRUTH
FOR A LIFE OF WISDOM

For the LORD gives wisdom;
from his mouth come knowledge and understanding. **PROVERBS 2:6**

AS WE SAW IN THE LAST CHAPTER, we can't know things (not even *ourselves*), only by looking within. We are not isolated individuals, free to determine reality in a vacuum. We are porous creatures, fluidly formed by others and forming them in return. We are profoundly shaped by our "situatedness"; what surrounds us; what comes into us, whether it be air or water or ideas. Peter Leithart puts it this way:

> Even at the most elementary level, we learn by taking the world in . . . Our brains, like our mouths and bellies, feed on the world. Learning is feasting, a taking-in of the world so that it becomes us, coursing through our brains the way nutrients flow through our blood.[1]

Our sources of intake are vitally important. They can make us healthy, or they can make us sick. Bad intake can make us unwise. Good intake—from trustworthy sources of truth—can make us wise, inoculating us against viruses of deception and error. That's what the second part of this book is about: a guide to healthier habits of information intake in an increasingly confusing age; a proposal for how we might orient our lives toward wisdom.

What Wisdom Is and Isn't

Wisdom is not knowledge. Nor is it information. This is abundantly clear in a world where we have more knowledge and information than ever, but less wisdom. To simply accumulate more knowledge is not to be wise. Robots will one day have far more knowledge than the smartest humans (if they don't already). But robots will never be wiser than humans. Wisdom is not a matter of mere data processing; there's no algorithm for it. Wisdom is also not necessarily the end result of education (though it certainly can be). Some of the most learned people in the world are not wise, and some of the wisest people in the world are not educated. Wisdom is knowing what *to do* with knowledge gained through various means of education: how to apply knowledge and information in everyday life; how to discern if something is true or not; how to live well in light of truth gained. Wisdom is not merely knowing the right answers. It's about living rightly. It's about determining *which* right answer is best. It's a moral orientation: a developed sense and intuition for discerning right and wrong, real and fake, truth and falsehood; the ability to weigh greater and lesser goods and make complex decisions involving multiple, sometimes competing truths. Wisdom is not something you can Google or download in one fell swoop. It is accumulated over time and through experience.

Wisdom and knowledge do have a symbiotic relationship. We can become more or less wise depending on the good or bad knowledge we take in. But the more wisdom we have, the better we become at filtering out bad knowledge and turning good knowledge into spiritual nutrition. Wisdom is sort of like a healthy kidney: it retains what is nutritious as it filters out the waste. A. W. Tozer compares wisdom to a vitamin, in that "it does not nourish a body in itself, but if not present, nothing will nourish the body. . . . A vitamin will make everything else work."[2]

But wisdom is not a vitamin you can purchase at CVS. There is no human doctor who can prescribe it—and this is key. As James puts it in the Bible, true wisdom is "from above," not below (James 3:17). It is the God-created (Prov. 8:22–32), God-given (Prov. 2:6), God-fearing (Prov. 1:7), God-oriented (Prov. 3:5–8) ability to synthesize, filter, evaluate, and apply information in ways that lead to right judgments and overall flourishing. We cannot be wise apart from God. God is the standard, the definition, the source, and the keeper of wisdom. But he's not greedy with it. He's happy to give it to us if only we ask (James 1:5).

This, however, is the struggle. Asking requires humility, and we want to believe we can be wise without God. To bypass God in pursuit of wisdom, however, is a fast track to folly. Just ask Adam and Eve. Only when we acknowledge God and submit to his sovereign rule can we begin to be wise. Little in this book will make sense unless you accept this premise.

What the "Wisdom Pyramid" Is and Isn't

The Wisdom Pyramid is a visual aid to help us understand what sorts of knowledge categories are reliable sources of truth and conducive to wisdom. Though inspired by the Food Pyramid in visual orientation and in offering "guidance for a healthy diet," the Wisdom Pyramid is unlike the Food Pyramid in a few important ways.

In the Food Pyramid, each "food group" is important for a "balanced diet." You need to eat food from all the groups in order to stay healthy. In the Wisdom Pyramid, this isn't necessarily the case. Only the two bottom sections of the Wisdom Pyramid are absolutely essential. The sections closer to the top *can* be healthy knowledge sources and often point to truth in their own ways, but it wouldn't be accurate to say you "need" them in order to be wise. There were plenty of wise people before the onset of the Internet, after all. Wisdom might benefit from a diversity of sources, but it doesn't *need* "balance" in the same way a living human body does. For example, if we only had the Bible to "feed" on to gain wisdom, we'd be okay, but *only* eating food from the "bread group" would ultimately make our bodies sickly.

As in the Food Pyramid, the hierarchical structure of the Wisdom Pyramid is important (though not in the same sense, as noted above). Two things are important to note about the structure of the Wisdom Pyramid: From the bottom up, it goes from most enduring (the eternal Word) to most fleeting (the here-and-gone social media post). From the bottom up, it also goes from most directly mediated by God (his spoken word to us in Scripture) to least directly mediated by God (machine-directed social media algorithms). It goes from clearer and more reliable communication of truth at the bottom to less clear, less reliable sources at the top, where truth is possible but requires more discernment to find.

The bottom sections of the pyramid are, therefore, more crucial priorities in our everyday knowledge habits than the top sections. The problem, of course, is that we've largely flipped the priority order today, with the most fleeting and human sources now occupying our epistemological foundation. But that foundation is like sinking sand. We need something more durable. We need an unwavering, unchanging, eternally trustworthy source of wisdom—something against which all other sources are measured. Millennia of human experience have shown that we find this in the very word of God.

The Wisdom Pyramid is not a comprehensive program for spiritual wellness or a life hack for optimized living in the digital age. I'm not a guru, and this book is humbly submitted mostly to steer you to sources *more trustworthy than I am*. My goal is simply to shine a non-exhaustive spotlight on a few vital, trustworthy, life-giving sources of truth to help you wisely navigate the chaos of the information age.

Chapter 4

THE BIBLE

Blessed is the man
    who walks not in the counsel of the wicked,
nor stands in the way of sinners,
    nor sits in the seat of scoffers;
but his delight is in the law of the LORD,
    and on his law he meditates day and night.
He is like a tree
    planted by streams of water
that yields its fruit in its season,
    and its leaf does not wither.
In all that he does, he prospers. PSALM 1:1-3

I WILL ALWAYS REMEMBER my dad's Bible. During my years as a kid, it was a fixture in our house: thick, black leather-bound, with gold leaf edges; stuffed full of church bulletins, Scripture memory cards, and who knows what else. The well-worn pages were adorned with underlined verses, variously hued highlighted sections, and scribbled marginalia. I saw dad with it almost every day—studying during his quiet time, preparing a Sunday school lesson, or maybe leading our family in a dinnertime devotional. The presence of Dad's Bible nearby was a comfort. I think it made the Bible more credible to me that, for my dad, it wasn't just a prop to bring to church on Sundays. It was his beloved source of guidance for everyday life.

And it wasn't just my dad. Growing up, I saw so many family members and friends who loved and were changed by the Bible. And so was I. My life was full of the Bible: learning Old Testament stories on flannelgraph in Sunday school, memorizing the order of the Bible's sixty-six books in Vacation Bible School, doing "sword drills" in Awana, memorizing the "Romans Road," singing songs that went,

> The B-I-B-L-E
> Yes that's the book for me!
> I stand alone on the Word of God:
> the B-I-B-L-E!

The Bible was the book that shaped my life more than anything else, which is odd looking back on it: a freckled, strawberry blonde Oklahoma kid being profoundly shaped by an ancient collection of Jewish literature and two-thousand-year-old Mediterranean letters. But I was, and I am. And my story isn't unique. The Bible has been a treasured source of truth and life all over the world, across countless generations. It manages to speak to the soccer mom in San Diego as much as to the truck driver in Taipei; it guides the life of a skateboarding teenager in 2020 Buenos Aires as much as it did the blacksmith in 1520 Liverpool. Everywhere you go in the world, people who share almost nothing else in common can say in unison: "The B-I-B-L-E, Yes, that's the book for me!" This can be said of no other book in the world. No other source of truth is as universally beloved and consistently cross-cultural as the Christian Bible. And this is why it should be the base layer of any Wisdom Pyramid.

Our Daily Bread

In the Food Pyramid of my childhood, the "bread group" was the foundational layer. And despite the ebbs and flows of the popularity of grains and gluten in various diet trends, its importance in the human diet is universal across cultures and history. Bread = survival.

So it is with the Bible. Is it any wonder that a popular daily Bible devotional is called *Our Daily Bread*? Jesus himself made the connection when he quoted Scripture to respond to Satan's temptation: "It is written, 'Man shall not live by bread alone, but by every word that comes from the mouth of God'" (Matt. 4:4).

If we are to become wise, our information diet must begin with the Bible. It must be our solid foundation, as well as the grid through which all other sources are tested. In a world of information overload, the Bible is graciously concise and yet comprehensive. In a world where information is fleeting and unreliable, the Bible is an ancient book that endures in every age—the bestselling book of history that has been read, preached, probed, and treasured by billions across the centuries. And in a world of "to each their own" truth, where one's inner compass is supposedly a trustworthy guide, the Bible represents an infinitely more reliable source of knowledge and truth: God himself.

The Bible is our most important source of wisdom because it is literally the eternal God—the standard and source of all truth—revealing himself. What a miraculous thing! Yet sadly many of us are bored by it, struggling to read it habitually, if at all. Our Bibles collect dust in a dark corner of our rooms while our Facebook feeds are constantly refreshed. When most of us start our days (myself included!), we read emails and tweets before we read the words of God.

And we wonder why we are struggling with wisdom. Today's post-truth world is like a claustrophobic escape room where we are all frantically fiddling with things on the floor, hoping they'll unlock an exit—all the while ignoring a hidden-in-plain-sight book that has the instructions we need. It's right there, waiting to be opened; waiting to liberate us from the rabbit trails and dead ends of a world of self-made "truth."

Uncreated Wisdom

Human, temporal wisdom only exists because God exists and graciously reveals himself to us. The Gospel of John opens by declaring:

> In the beginning was the Word, and the Word was with God, and the Word was God. He was in the beginning with God. All things were made through him, and without him was not any thing made that was made. In him was life, and the life was the light of men. (John 1:1–4)

These verses associate the eternal wisdom of God with words: words that create; words that illuminate; the uncreated Logos who became flesh in the person of Jesus Christ, "in whom are hidden all the treasures of wisdom and knowledge" (Col. 2:3). In 1 Corinthians 2, Paul says the gospel he imparts is "not a wisdom of this age or of the rulers of this age" (v. 6), but is rather "a secret and hidden wisdom of God, which God decreed before the ages for our glory" (v. 7).

The Bible makes known to us, temporal creatures in fixed places and times, some of this hidden and eternal wisdom. It is God initiating a conversation with us, if we have ears to hear. "The whole course of the biblical narrative is structured as a dialogue," John Frame writes in *The Doctrine of the Word of God*. "God speaks, man responds. The course of subsequent history is the result of man's response to God's word."[1]

If the Bible is anything less than God's personal words to us, then treating it as the foundation of wisdom makes little sense. If it's just an ancient collection of sacred texts created by humans to propagate a particular religion, the Bible would be of little importance. But the Bible is not just a book. It is God's very words to us. When we read the Bible, we are encountering God himself.

Scripture's Authority

The inextricable link between God's word and God himself means that if we love God, we will love his word. If we fear God, we fear his word. If we view Jesus Christ as authoritative, we also view Scripture as authoritative (as Jesus himself did).[2] When God speaks, we are obligated to obey. His speech, and only his, is supremely authoritative. And Scripture is his speech.

But we humans hate authority. We don't like subjecting ourselves to anyone other than ourselves. We like to think (as we saw in chapter 3) *we* are all we need to figure out how to flourish in the world. Adam's original sin was a proud intellectual self-sufficiency, what J. I. Packer describes as the "ability to solve all life's problems without reference to the word of God."[3] True faith, argues Packer, means giving up the notion of intellectual autonomy and recognizing that "true wisdom begins with a willingness to treat God's Word as possessing final authority."[4] Man is not the measure of all things. God is.

God's word is our most important and indisputable authority. This is not to say it is the *only* authority. R. C. Sproul notes that the Reformation notion of *sola Scriptura* does not mean the Bible is the *only* authority for the Christian, but that it is the only *infallible* authority.[5] Popes, councils, church tradition, pastors, scholars with PhDs, and every other human source is fallible, but Scripture is infallible—for the simple reason that God himself is infallible.

This is important because some Christian traditions place the authority of Scripture on equal footing with other authorities. Roman Catholicism, for example, places church tradition on authoritative par with Scripture. Some liberal Christians place human reason on par with Scripture's authority, suggesting our contemporary values and subjective interpretations ultimately determine the Bible's meaning. But both these approaches break down because they place too much authority in the flawed interpretations of men.

Again, this is not to say church tradition and human reason (among other things) are not *valuable* authorities; it's just that they are *lesser* authorities than the authority of Scripture. This is why, as we move on in this book and look at other sources of truth, knowledge, and information that can help us become wise, it's important to measure them all against Scripture—the *only infallible* source of truth.

But is Scripture really *infallible*? Wasn't it written by fallible humans? Isn't it full of seeming errors and contradictions? These are common objections to treating Scripture as an ultimate epistemological authority. Answering them sufficiently would require much more space than I have here. But the short response is that the focus must be on God's infallibility and perfect original communication to us, not on the imperfection of human copyists, translators, and interpreters. Sproul puts it succinctly when he says, "When orthodoxy confesses the infallibility of Scripture it is not confessing anything about the intrinsic infallibility of men. Rather the confession rests its confidence on the integrity of God."[6]

What a relief. We can trust in Scripture—that it is all "breathed out by God" (2 Tim. 3:16)—because we trust in *God*. It's not about our certainty or our perfect understanding. It's about God's perfection and his sufficiency in not only revealing his truth to us but also in translating it to us by the power of the Holy Spirit.

God's Translator: The Holy Spirit

In 1 Corinthians 2, Paul says his speech and his message "were not in plausible words of wisdom, but in demonstration of the Spirit and of power, so that your faith might not rest in the wisdom of men but in the power of God" (vv. 4–5).

Our faith rests in the power of God, who allows us to hear and process his words in such a way that it leads to faith and understanding. There are rational reasons to believe Scripture is true, but ultimately "our full persuasion and assurance of [Scripture's] infallible truth and divine authority" comes from "the inward work of the Holy Spirit bearing witness by and with the Word in our hearts," as the Westminster Confession of Faith declares.[7]

The Holy Spirit inspired the writing and illuminates the reading of Scripture, such that "the author of the text opens the text to us."[8] Packer writes:

> Without the Spirit's help there can be no grasp of the message of Scripture, no conviction of the truth of Scripture, and no faith in the God of Scripture. Without the Spirit, nothing is possible but spiritual blindness and unbelief . . . Our God-given textbook is a closed book till our God-given Teacher opens it to us.[9]

The hidden wisdom of God is revealed to us by the Spirit, as Paul writes in 1 Corinthians 2, and "no one comprehends the things of God except the Spirit of God" (v. 11). In the Reformation, Calvin described a *testimonium Spiritus Sancti internum*—the internal testimony of the Holy Spirit. Writing in his *Institutes*, he said:

Our conviction of the truth of Scripture must be derived from a higher source than human conjectures, judgments, or reasons; namely, the secret testimony of the Spirit. . . . The testimony of the Spirit is superior to reason. For as God alone can properly bear witness to his own words, so these words will not obtain full credit on the hearts of men, until they are sealed by the inward testimony of the Spirit.[10]

Similarly, Jonathan Edwards described a "spiritual taste" which "true Christians have to guide them and give them discernment by the Spirit of God."[11] This "spiritual taste" does not create new meaning from God's word but helps a reader discern the proper reading and application of it. "It removes the prejudices of a depraved appetite and leads the thoughts naturally in the right way," wrote Edwards. "It casts light on the Word of God and causes the true meaning most naturally to come to mind, because there is a harmony between the disposition and relish of a sanctified soul and the true meaning of the rules of God's Word."[12]

Importantly, the work of the Spirit as relates to Scripture is *not* to make new revelation but to illuminate what has already been revealed. We are on dangerous ground when we claim the Spirit has led us to some new revelation or insight beyond what is in Scripture. "The Spirit is not the prompter of fanciful spiritualizing," writes Packer. "The only meaning to which He bears witness is that which each text actually has in the organism of Scripture."[13]

But what does it mean that there are so many divergent and contradictory readings of Scripture? Is the Holy Spirit translating God's words differently to different people? What are the marks of a Spirit-driven reading and application of Scripture as opposed to a fleshly, human approach?

Five Principles for Rightly Handling Scripture

Rightly handling Scripture is a massive and important topic. What follows is obviously just skimming the surface. Many other helpful resources exist on the topic, but in this space I want to describe just a few key principles for making the most of this important foundation for wisdom.[14]

1. SCRIPTURE SHOULD SPEAK TO *ALL* OF LIFE

We can sometimes look at Scripture as a resource that only speaks to the state of our soul or offers tips for a moral life. But Scripture is not something to compartmentalize as one among many resources to evoke when certain situations arise. Because it is the word of God, who is Lord over all, Scripture speaks to us about everything: money, sex, family, art, science, justice, and politics, to name a few. To properly handle the Bible is to acknowledge that it should inform everything in our lives, no matter who we are, what we do, or how we feel. Furthermore, rather than seeing the Bible as threatened by or in competition with other disciplines (like science or philosophy or economics), we should see how Scripture works in tandem with reason to illuminate the mysteries of the world. We should not see the Bible as a manual for how to escape this world, but rather as a book of wisdom for, in part, applying God's revealed truth to all of life *now*. We should "think biblically about everything," as an advertising slogan for Biola University once stated.[15] Scripture should be both the foundation and impetus for all our knowledge pursuits.

2. SCRIPTURE SHOULD DEFINE YOUR PARADIGM
(NOT THE OTHER WAY AROUND)

You might be thinking, *If to love the Bible is to become wise, then why are so many Bible-loving people so awful and unwise—using the Bible in self-serving ways to defend ignorance, justify bias, and perpetuate fear and loathing?* The answer is that they are *using* the Bible. They aren't coming to the Bible to be shaped by it; they are coming to the Bible to shape it into what they want it to be. We see it in politics all the time: "Christians" in both parties appeal to the Bible to justify their political stances. We see it in our own lives too. All of us tend to like the parts of Scripture that support our paradigms while we ignore or downplay the parts that threaten our status quo. But bad things happen when we start shaping Scripture around *us* rather than ourselves around Scripture. We must always be on guard against force-fitting Scripture into boxes of our liking.

3. SCRIPTURE IS VALUABLE AS A WHOLE, NOT JUST THE PARTS

We often approach Scripture in a piecemeal fashion, pulling bits out of context to defend this or that position or to make some topical point. Many preachers perpetuate this by using random verses here or there to prove their topical points, rather than deriving their points from careful study of Scripture as a whole. But context is everything in Bible study. The truth of any given verse becomes clearer when we see it in the larger context. We get the most out of the Bible when we read it in big chunks and grasp its grand narrative. The Bible is a cohesive *narrative*, after all, not just a collection of random quotables for your #Blessed life. This means we must avoid picking and choosing only the parts we like, or creating canons-within-canons where we favor some parts of Scripture over others (e.g., the New Testament over the Old Testament, the scientifically feasible over the supernatural/miracles, the "red letters" of Christ's quotes over everything else). As Frame says, "Since Scripture is God's personal word, *all* of it is authoritative . . . not just those parts that we find attractive, cogent, relevant, or culturally respectable."[16]

4. SCRIPTURE SHOULD SPARK WORSHIP AND OBEDIENCE

We must "be doers of the word, and not hearers only" (James 1:22). Our lives should be beautifully transformed by the Bible because we *obey* what it says. Part of this is acknowledging that the Bible should engage not only our minds, but also our hearts, leading us to *love* the Lord and trust him more and more. We read the Bible to know its author, to behold the beauty and glory of Christ. As Puritan writer John Owen put it, "The glory of Scripture is that it is the great, indeed, the only outward means for us to know the glory of Christ."[17] The wisdom of Scripture is thus intimately tied to worship and love. We obey God's word because we love Jesus (John 14:21). We are *doers* of the Word because we are *lovers* of God. Our time in the Bible should ideally pair with time in prayer, speaking back to God in love and gratitude even as he speaks to us. If the first step of wisdom is fear of God, the second step is to have our hearts "subdued by *piety*," wrote Augustine, "and not to run in the face of Holy Scripture. . . . We must rather think and believe that whatever is there written, even though it be hidden, is better and truer than anything we could devise by our own wisdom."[18] Indeed, wisdom comes when we are grateful for and defer to God's word above our own instincts, when we "trust in the LORD with all [our] heart, and do not lean on [our] own understanding" (Prov. 3:5)

5. SCRIPTURE DOESN'T HAVE TO MAKE COMPLETE SENSE

Gaining wisdom from Bible study requires a deep intellectual humility. We are dealing with the words of an omniscient God, after all, revealed to writers in ancient cultural contexts. If it all makes perfect sense, and we have answers and resolutions for every knotty paradox and mystery the Bible raises, something is wrong. It is arrogant and dangerous to believe every mystery of Scripture or seeming inconsistency can be smoothly ironed out. Often this leads to heresy. Beware the scholar who asserts a definitive formula for understanding the Trinity, the incarnation, the atonement, or other difficult doctrines. A healthier approach is to be okay with some measure of "I don't know." This doesn't mean we turn off our brains, throw up our hands, and tolerate theological fuzziness. Rather, the difficulties of Scripture should invite us to even more rigorous and precise examination, going deeper and wider in our study as lifelong learners, not because we have to know everything God knows, but because the more immersed we are in Scripture, the nearer we feel to his sweet presence. "We do not understand everything in Scripture," Frame writes, "but we understand much, by God's grace. And what we understand becomes the foundation of our lives, our only comfort in life and death."[19]

Treasuring the Gift

This morning I sat in my reading chair and pulled my eleven-month-old son, Chet, into my lap for some Bible reading. He's wiggly, distracted, and more interested in eating or tearing the pages than in hearing me read the words. (Ironically, a few weeks ago he ripped out an entire page of Proverbs as I read the words of Proverbs 23:15: "My son, if your heart is wise, my heart too will be glad"!) Despite his wiggles this morning, I found myself full of gratitude and moved to tears as I read. The Bible is such a treasure. Such a gift!

What a gift it is to be able to read this text to my son—the same text my father read to me and that so many generations of fathers and mothers read to their children. What a gift to have this physical book in my lap, well-worn and full of marked-up pages, like my dad's Bible was growing up—a treasured refuge to return to day after day in every peak and valley of life. What a gift to have this infallible, holy source of truth in a world where we are weary of untruths and beleaguered by untrustworthy information on every side, including in our own deceptive hearts.

Do we stop enough to consider how mind-blowing it is that God revealed himself to us in this way, speaking words to us about himself when he could have remained silent? As my colleague Matt Smethurst has noted, God could have left us in our ignorance, undeserving sinners that we are:

> But he didn't. He peeled back the curtain. And then opened his holy mouth. Any authentic knowledge of God hinges on his generous self-disclosure to us. Only through his words can we discover who he is, what he's like, what he's after, and how we can know him. This ought to humble us deeply. The Bible you possess is evidence that God loves you and wants a relationship with you. No matter who you are or how many times you've spurned his love, he is still moving toward you, still talking to you—still befriending you—through a book.[20]

How remarkable. The gracious self-disclosure of God, through a book, should daily inspire in us the sort of gratitude and praise we see in Psalm 19. God's word revives the soul and makes wise the simple (v. 7); it rejoices the heart and enlightens the eyes (v. 8); it is more desirable than gold and sweeter than honey (v. 10). We should have the fervor of John Wesley, who once said, "O give me that book! At any price, give me the book of God!"[21]

Do we treasure the Bible this way? Do we delight in it and meditate on it day and night, such that we become, as the psalmist writes, like a tree planted by streams of water, robust and sturdy and fruitful rather than fleeting like chaff? John Owen rightly observed that one's spiritual vitality is manifest in a healthy appetite for Scripture: "If you have no appetite for God's word then your spiritual life is in a bad state."[22] Do we wake in the morning with a hunger for the "sweeter than honey" daily sustenance of Scripture, full of God-given nutrients that have fed billions of people over thousands of years, or do we instead go to the vending machines of our smartphones, snacking on whatever addictive candy appeals to our tastes in the moment?

Tragically, our Wisdom Pyramids are often upside down. What should be the base level—God's eternal word—is often relegated to the "use sparingly" top. Meanwhile, what should really be at the "use sparingly" top—man's ephemeral words (i.e., social media)—often occupies our foundation. And we wonder why we are going crazy.

But the Bible is there for us, thanks be to God. It's a treasure that isn't even buried. The most trustworthy and important source of truth that humanity has ever known is easily found. It's in the drawer in your hotel room. It's in the app store. It's on Amazon. It's probably on your shelf, or your grandma's shelf.

Open it. Download it. Read it. Treasure it. Obey it. Become wise.

DISCUSSION QUESTIONS

1. What habits or rhythms have worked for you in making Scripture more central in your day-to-day life?

2. What are some resources (books, commentaries, videos, podcasts, etc.) you have found that have energized your Bible reading and study, or that have made the Bible more exciting and approachable to you?

3. What does it look like to let Scripture shape you rather than you attempting to shape Scripture? Where do you see examples of the latter, and why is it problematic?

Chapter 5

THE CHURCH

*Let us consider how to stir up one another to love and good
works, not neglecting to meet together, as is the habit of
some, but encouraging one another, and all the more as
you see the Day drawing near.* HEBREWS 10:24-25

RECENT HEADLINES ABOUT the church have been dominated by the
word *leaving*. The narrative has been that people—especially young
people—in Western culture are leaving the church, finding it unnecessary or counterproductive for their spiritual quest.

The reasons are understandable. Churches are full of sinful, work-
in-progress people, after all, and problems inevitably arise. Interper-
sonal conflicts. Leadership scandals. Hypocrisy. Abuses of authority.
#ChurchToo. Cover-ups. Apathy about injustice and the plight of
the marginalized. Marrying faith too close to partisan politics. For a
lot of "good vibes only" young people who have been reared on technology that allows them to filter out anything difficult or annoying,
church and its motley crew of often-frustrating people might seem
like more trouble than it's worth.

Furthermore, many Western Christians have been raised in a faith
that puts heavy emphasis on the individual ("personal relationship with

Jesus") and little (if any) emphasis on the communal. If Christianity is mostly about doing your own thing with Jesus, then leaving church becomes easy to justify. If church *adds* something to one's personal spiritual walk, then great. But if it is a hassle or a hindrance, just ditch it. You can love Jesus without loving the church . . . or so the logic goes.

But as much as church seems like an easy "pass" in today's world, the reality is it can be an indispensable source of stability and growth; a treasure trove of communal and Spirit-infused wisdom that we'd be foolish to neglect. The church, the *people* of God, is second only to the Bible, the *word* of God, as a source of reliable and transformative wisdom. Especially in our unwise age, attaching oneself to the church—the global, growing, two-thousand-plus-years-old body of Jesus Christ on earth—can be like finding a lighthouse when you're lost in a raging sea. A faithful, Christ-centered church and its wisdom-infusing patterns of worship is increasingly a refuge for those being pummeled by the maelstrom of our digital era. It certainly is for me. By the time Sunday rolls around each week, I feel desperate for it: desperate to be around real, flesh-and-blood community after spending my week mostly interacting with people through screens; desperate to be transported from the fickle and fleeting debates of social media and into a space of worship that glimpses the eternal.

Rather than running *away* from the church in these confusing and chaotic times, people should be running *to* the church. Here are a few reasons why.

The Wisdom of Community in an Individualistic Age

If the voice of God in Scripture is the voice of eternal wisdom, then knowing Scripture is knowing wisdom. That's why Scripture (as we saw in the last chapter) is the absolute foundation of any wisdom diet. It's the only perfect source of truth. But part of knowing Scripture well is knowing it in community. This is one reason the church is so important. We can read and enjoy the Bible on our own, totally apart from a church, and unfortunately for some people in the world this may be their only option. But the ancient Bible isn't always easy to understand for contemporary readers, and individualistic interpretations of it ("what it means to me") can lead to heretical places.

The church is an interpretive *community*, where collective wisdom across church history and in various polity structures (denominations, elder boards, membership) provides guardrails against errant theology. The church brings fullness and focus to our understanding and application of God's truth, in ways that go deeper than what a "just me and Jesus" approach can provide.

Our post-truth age pitches the individual self as the primary source of truth: "follow your heart," "live your truth," and so forth. As we saw in chapter 3, authorities of every kind outside the self are now being questioned. And yet we follow our heart—which is "deceitful above all things, and desperately sick" (Jer. 17:9)—at our peril, becoming subject to the whims and contradictions of our fickle emotions. It sounds freeing to just "live your truth," without the restrictive boundaries of moral police and stodgy institutions. But in reality it's a burden.

It may seem counterintuitive, but committing yourself to a church, even if it's not perfectly fit to you (as tempting as this is), is freeing. A church community frees you from the crushing weight of self-obsession. It frees you to be part of something bigger than yourself, with people who are not like you. It frees you from the bias-confirming bubbles of only being exposed to like-minded people who always affirm but never challenge you. It frees you from the burden of being accountable only to yourself: what *you* believe, how *you* like to worship, how *you* interpret the Bible, how *you* want to live and so on. When we are the only authority on these things, it's hard to become wise.

Church community may be challenging, but it's the sort of challenging we need in order to grow. It's a community where we encourage and "stir up one another to love and good works" (Heb. 10:24); a community of Spirit-enabled transformation, where gifts are given to individual members for the building up of the collective body (1 Corinthians 12). It's a community that helps us see our blind spots and areas of needed growth; a diverse community of walking, talking, living examples of Christlikeness we can observe and emulate.

Going it alone will get you only so far. Accountability only to your own "authority" will probably lead you to spiritual sickness. We need community if we are to become wise. Communities of all sorts can help us in this: our blood family, our friend groups, our professional and civic associations, our "Inklings-esque" cohorts of artists and thinkers. All of these provide some measure of accountability and spurring-on that can help us become wise. As C. S. Lewis says, "The next best thing to becoming wise oneself is to live in a circle of those who are."[1]

So surround yourself with others who are wise. Give yourself to community, even if it's uncomfortable. Almost every community will help you become wiser than you would be alone. But a church community—a group committed to pursuing holiness *collectively* and more interested in glorifying God than in celebrating the "authentic" self—can offer particularly valuable nutrition for a healthy wisdom diet.

The Wisdom of God-Centered Rhythms in a Me-Centered Age

The weekly rituals of church worship orient our lives around God and his wisdom. When every moment of our iWorld existence conditions us to celebrate the self, the church boldly celebrates something bigger and grander and more compelling. In an age of nauseating narcissism where everyone clamors for stardom and Instagram likes, the church humbles us and weekly reminds us: this is not about you. This is about God. You are welcome here, you are wanted, your presence in the body is important. You are part of the story. But God is the star, not you. What a freeing and wonderful thing.

A healthy church proclaims a message that is radically God-centered, not me-centered. Trevin Wax puts it this way:

> Expressive individualism would have us look deep into our hearts to discover our inner essence and express that to the world. But the gospel shows how the depths of our hearts are steeped in sin; it claims that what we need most is not expression, but redemption. The world says we should look inward, while the gospel says to look upward. In an expressive individualist society, that message is countercultural.[2]

Upward, not inward. Redemption, not expression. These are just some of the radical alternatives the church offers our me-centered age. In a world that is constantly on the move, church worship forces us to be still. In a "quick to speak" world that is deafeningly loud, church worship allows us to sit quietly and *listen*, basking in God's word preached and his wisdom imparted. In a world where we spend way too much time talking about *ourselves*—on social media, blogs, YouTube, and so forth—church worship allows us to talk about God and to God. We sing of his attributes, his love and mercy toward us. We declare it in liturgy, creeds, and prayers. We are shaped by his story, in Bible readings, preaching, baptism, the Lord's Supper, confession, singing together, and other regular rituals.

Wisdom isn't just about concepts. It's about the *orientations* of our time and energy, the *postures* that shape our hearts, often on subconscious levels. Prayer, for example, is a crucial habit for gaining wisdom—not only because the Bible says gaining wisdom can be as simple as praying for it (James 1:5, Col. 1:9), but also because the *posture* of prayer itself cultivates wisdom. Every prayer is a rebuttal to the "look within" logic of our age. To pray is to acknowledge that we *don't* have all the answers in ourselves. We *don't* have sufficient wisdom to make complex decisions. We must humbly turn to God, the giver of wisdom (Prov. 2:6), seeking his guidance in all things. We are utterly reliant on him.

The church helps habituate us to these crucial counter-formational practices, like prayer. We neglect them at our peril, especially in a world so apt at forming us to be *unwise*. As Mark Sayers puts it in *Reappearing Church*:

> Do we sense the possibilities of embodied and enfleshed Christian community in a time of disembodied isolation? In a time of anxiety and mental exhaustion, are we seeing the rich traditions of prayer, contemplation, and meditation upon God as antidotes to our exhausted brains? In a time of social fracturing and cultural polarization, do we understand the powerful place that exists at the communion table?[3]

I also find that the *annual* rhythms of the church calendar provide a coherent ordering to time that we need in an unstructured age. Today, time tends to be ordered around whatever is currently trending in the news, whatever hashtag day it might be (e.g., #NationalDonutDay, #InternationalWomensDay, #WorldBookDay), or whatever commercial "holiday" it is where we are encouraged to buy stuff (e.g., Valentine's Day, Mother's Day and Father's Day). In contrast, time in the Christian tradition orients us around God and his story. Advent is a period of anticipation and longing as we ponder Christ's incarnation. Christmas is a feast for celebrating the gift of Christ's coming to earth. Lent is a season of simplicity and meditation as we prepare our hearts to remember Christ's sacrifice. Maundy Thursday, Good Friday, Holy Saturday, and Easter Sunday are the four-day climax of the Christian year, but sadly many Christians are more familiar with the "secular holy week" of Thanksgiving, Black Friday, Small Business Saturday, and Cyber Monday.

The ancient church calendar rhythms and weekly worship rhythms of the local church can be powerful counter-formational forces in our lives. Like anything, it's all about regularity and habit. Occasional or when-convenient appearances at church will hardly shape us. But showing up weekly and immersing yourself in a church's "not-about-me" orientation can do wonders for your spiritual sanity in an unwise age.

The Wisdom of Limitations in a Limitless Age

If the "anything is possible," too-much-of-everything nature of our age is making us sickly and unwise, one of the greatest gifts the church can offer is focus, grounding, and limitation.

Academy Award-winning cinematographer Emmanuel Lubezki once said, "Art is made of constraints. When you don't have any, you go crazy, because everything is possible."[4] This sentiment could easily be applied to life in general. Change the word "art" in that quote to "life," and it still works. We go crazy in life when everything is possible. We don't know where to look, where to go, what to trust, what path to take. If every direction is possible we end up going nowhere. This is where the church, functioning as a community of accountability and limitation, is actually *freeing* for any who commit to it.

At its best, the nuclear family functions in this way too. It is our first community—our most proximate and continuous teacher in life. While families take on various shapes and sizes, and various degrees of health, this micro-community represents the people most likely to shape who we become. One's nuclear family is a God-given gift of *limitation*. Rather than free agents who roam the planet without aim or attachment, we are rooted, enmeshed, and formed within this *particular* group of people we didn't choose. The *givenness* of a nuclear family is a gift we should cherish and uphold—especially in an age sometimes prone to pitch "global citizenship" as somehow more compelling than local membership.

Committing to a local church family—like embracing one's place in one's given nuclear family—means committing to *this particular* family, *this particular* place, *this particular* outpost of God's kingdom. It is a narrowing down of our field of limitless choices. But far from shrinking our world, this limitation is freeing. To land in a church and to be grounded there, to be *accountable* there, provides a spiritual and relational stability that reduces the number of variables in life. It provides a defined plot of land where we can put down roots, grow, and be fruitful. It challenges the FOMO restlessness that tempts us to move so quickly from place to place that we never bear fruit anywhere.

The church also provides moral limitations. Rather than the burden of "everything is possible" morality, where right and wrong are in the eye of the beholder, the church—guided by Scripture and interpretive tradition—offers refreshing clarity on what is clearly okay and clearly not okay, and how to navigate the gray areas in between. These clarifying boundaries can be a gift to us, but we have to be willing to submit to them.

Recently the actor Chris Pratt, a churchgoing Christian in Hollywood, responded to complaints by lesbian actress Ellen Page that he attended an "infamously anti-LGBTQ" church. Seeking to distance himself from wherever his church might stand on biblical sexual ethics, he said this: "My faith is important to me but no church defines me or my life . . . My values define who I am."[5]

Sadly this approach—where one's personal values prevail if they conflict with one's church's position—is far too common. Such an approach rejects the gift a church can be when it functions as a higher authority than—and gracious limitation upon—the autonomous self. Do we really think "my values" are a more reliable source of truth than church teaching that has been consistent for centuries? If we do, then we've turned church into a consumer commodity that exists merely to serve our interests on our terms.

The reality is church is a source of truth precisely because it *doesn't* exist to serve our interests on our terms. It *doesn't* exist to agree with popular ideologies, affirm everyone's "authenticity," and shapeshift to avoid hurting anyone's feelings. The church exists to glorify God by making faithful, holy disciples of Jesus. Accepting the simplicity of that and joyfully committing to it provides a freeing focus in a limitless age.

The Wisdom of Embodied Community in an Ethereal Age

One of the greatest sources of folly in today's world is that we are increasingly living disembodied lives in ethereal space—pulled everywhere but grounded nowhere. Social media is attention whiplash. One minute we are drawn into some drama happening in Washington, DC. The next minute we see a friend's photo from Fiji, followed by a headline about political unrest in Hong Kong, and so forth. We bounce from "place" to "place" without really being anywhere, least of all the actual place we inhabit. Lost in endless Twitter grievances and the insipid controversies that fuel

Internet life, we neglect the local people and tangible issues in our own backyard.

In the digital age we have the illusion of "connection" with our many social media followers, but we find ourselves lonely and unknown behind all the manipulative filters and layers of facade. We feel involved in causes and issues, but the limits of our #Hashtag activism only leave us frustrated. Constant exposure to the problems "out there"—through social media and news sites oriented more around bad news than good—gives us an apocalyptic picture of the darkness of the world, leaving us angry and depressed.

For all of human history prior to the onset of mass media about a century ago, humans troubled themselves with the problems nearest to them: first in their nuclear family/home/farm, then in their village or larger community, then (maybe) in their larger region or nation. That was usually as far as it went, and it was burdensome enough. Today it seems we spend *less* time on the tangible communities nearest to us—the people we actually live near and the problems we can actually help solve—than we do on the intangible, controversial headlines from the other side of the world. Our inflated focus on global *awareness* depletes our capacity for local *action*. It's of course valuable to be aware of the wider world *to some extent*, but there is wisdom in embracing the focus and limits of localism.

This is why a local church can be an antidote to our disembodied grief. It grounds us in tangible geographic reality and reminds us that we are embodied people, not just brains on sticks. We were made for physical connection with people in real places, not just informational connection through the mediation of screens. In a lonely, disembodied world, the church offers a beautiful alternative: an enfleshed community where the manipulative filters of life online fall away and you can be known in a truer sense, warts and all. It's a place where our struggles and weaknesses are harder to hide; a place where healing—emotional, spiritual, physical—can happen. It's a place where you can do physical things together: sing, stand, sit, kneel, hug, attempt awkward bro handshakes, even *eat and drink* the communion elements.

It's significant that Jesus gave us a *meal* as the central rite of Christian remembrance. He could have just told his disciples: "Remember the *idea* of me. Remember these theological *concepts* about me in your brain." Instead, he told them to "*do this* in remembrance of me" (1 Cor. 11:24) as he broke real bread and poured real wine. Take, eat. Take, drink. Physical actions. Jesus doesn't just want a relationship with us on the thought level. He wants us to commune with him, and one another, as *embodied beings.* He came as an incarnate, flesh-and-blood person who walked and talked and ate with us. God could have just sent us a PowerPoint presentation with five ideas to believe in order to be saved. Instead he sent a person. God in flesh, our hope divine.

A physical, in-flesh church can be a haven for us digital ghosts. However uncomfortable it is to do church with a couple hundred weird, smelly, not-like-me people whose hugs and handshakes are often awkward, the experience of embodied church can be a massive source of truth and hope in a lonely digital age.

The Wisdom of Continuity in a Constantly Changing Age

We live in an age of constant novelty. As we saw in chapter 2, our digital feeds filter reality to us in short bursts of *what's happening now*: breaking news headlines, trending videos, the latest meme. But all of it is fleeting and disposable. The past and the future are out of sight and mind. This is not a recipe for wisdom. It's a recipe for whiplash as we're tossed to and fro between the latest (and almost instantly outdated) philosophy, fashion, or fad. It's a recipe for fragmentation and disconnection, as we live unmoored from tradition and history, susceptible to whatever sales pitch speaks into our head at any given moment.

One of the beautiful things about being part of a church, and one of its greatest gifts to our generation, is that it grounds us in a bigger story—one that precedes us and will outlive us, where the past and the future matter as much (or more) than the present. In a presentist world where wisdom is shrunk to the narrow confines of *immediate relevance*, the church broadens horizons. It draws upon wisdom and truth from thousands of years ago and speaks to realities that will exist millions of years from now. It situates us within a story that crosses cultures and borders and transcends time and space. It invites the refugees of a relentlessly unstable world to take refuge in the practices and time-filtered wisdom of two millennia of Christian tradition.

Christian heritage is a treasure trove of time-tested truth we would do well to mine. There is a great cloud of witnesses who came before us and wrestled with many of the questions and trials we face today. It's important for contemporary Christians to avoid chronological snobbery, assuming our issues and insights are unique or new. To guard against this we should familiarize ourselves with our family of faith across time, drawing from and building upon their wisdom. We should read the theology of John Chrysostom and John Calvin, Augustine and Athanasius. We should read biographies of faithful Christ-followers from bygone eras: Martin Luther, William Tyndale, William Wilberforce, Phillis Wheatley, Harriet Tubman, Hannah More, Father Damien, Elisabeth Elliot, Charles Spurgeon, Susanna Wesley, and many others.

Ultimately the value of continuity in church history is that it releases us from the burden of chasing relevance. Every generation need not reinvent the wheel. We simply need to know our story and place ourselves within it, understanding that the strength of the church is continuity rather than constant reinvention, transcendence rather than trendiness. We need churches to be less concerned with being "up on the times" than being connected to the timeless. We need churches that are shaped by the gospel more than by the zeitgeist.

At its best, the church takes us out of the uncertainty of the ephemeral and places us in the certainty of the eternal. It reminds us of our destiny and puts the latest social media obsessions into perspective. Everything ever tweeted and the most-viewed viral videos will be forgotten ashes in the embers of history, but the church will remain.

That's why it's a massively important staple of any wisdom diet.

DISCUSSION QUESTIONS

1. If we have the Bible—and it is an infallible source of truth—then why do we also need the church? What role does a local church, and church tradition, play in terms of our gleaning wisdom from Scripture?

2. Why is prayer so pivotal as a habit for gaining wisdom?

3. What would you say to someone who questions the logic of church as the second most important source for one's wisdom diet? Which of the arguments in this chapter do you think would be most compelling to a church skeptic?

Chapter 6

NATURE

The LORD by wisdom founded the earth;
by understanding he established the heavens;
by his knowledge the deeps broke open,
and the clouds drop down the dew. PROVERBS 3:19-20

NATURE CAN BE STUBBORN. The weather abides no "alternative facts." It is either snowing or it isn't. A flood, drought, or hurricane is a quick reminder that nature's unpredictable behavior cannot be escaped or manipulated.

I live in Southern California, where climate-controlled houses and air-conditioned cars give us a measure of mastery over summer's triple-digit temperatures or winter's atmospheric river storms. But we can't escape nature completely. A mudslide washes away parts of Highway 1, making it impassable. The Santa Ana winds will blow, causing us to cough on the air that "tastes like a stubbed out cigarette" as the poet Dana Gioia (aptly) says.[1] Months of no rain crisp the Sonoran landscape, making it ripe for autumn wildfires. The weather doesn't ask for our opinion.

Nature reminds us there is a world bigger than the one we've made.

A few years ago I saw a headline in the *Los Angeles Times* that sums it up well: "We may live in a post-truth era, but nature does not."[2]

Perhaps that's one of the reasons I've always loved nature—God's beautiful and terrifying creation. It is what it *is*, not what we want it to be. In a world where man thinks he is the measure of all things, nature begs to differ. There is a *givenness* to nature that is sanity in an insane world. It is there to sustain our lives, to be enjoyed, but also to challenge us, to put us in our place, and to impart to us wisdom—if we are willing to listen.

Why Nature Is a Source of Wisdom

Why look to nature for wisdom? Well, if it's true we become wiser by knowing God more, then it follows that we can know more about God, in part, by observing his creation—just as you can know things about Vincent van Gogh by examining his paintings or something about Martin Scorsese by watching his films.

But we have Scripture. Isn't that enough? It's true that Scripture is our supreme and only infallible source of knowledge of God. But here's the thing: Scripture *itself* tells us that wisdom can be found in God's creation. In Proverbs 8, personified "wisdom" says she was present with God before and during the creation of the world. "When he established the heavens, I was there," says wisdom (v. 27). "When he marked out the foundations of the earth, then I was beside him, like a master workman" (vv. 29–30). The world was created, literally, with wisdom. As one writer put it, "God programmed the world with wisdom. To use a computer analogy, wisdom is the operating system of the universe."[3]

Elsewhere in Scripture, we see that wisdom can be found by closely observing God's handiwork: "Go to the ant, O sluggard; consider her ways, and be wise" (Prov. 6:6); "But ask the beasts, and they will teach you; the birds of the heavens, and they will tell you; or the bushes of the earth, and they will teach you; and the fish of the sea will declare to you" (Job 12:7–8). Solomon was "wiser than all other men" (1 Kings 4:31), and part of this included broad knowledge of the natural world: "He spoke of trees, from the cedar that is in Lebanon to the hyssop that grows out of the wall. He spoke also of beasts, and of birds, and of reptiles, and of fish" (1 Kings 4:33).

To be sure, nature as a communicator of truth and wisdom is always imperfect and indirect. It is a ripple, a residue, a "first sketch" of the greater glory that awaits us, as C. S. Lewis says: "Nature is only the image, the symbol; but it is the symbol Scripture invites me to use. We are summoned to pass in through Nature, beyond her, into that splendour which she fitfully reflects."[4] Nature's glory is not an end unto itself. It's not a god to worship. It's a prism and amplifier of *God's* glory. It's a theater, a canvas, a cathedral, but God is always at center stage.

The Second Book

John Calvin described creation as a "large and splendid mansion gorgeously constructed and exquisitely furnished," and everything in it points to the builder.[5] Scripture itself talks in these terms. "The heavens declare the glory of God, and the sky above proclaims his handiwork" (Ps. 19:1). "For his invisible attributes, namely, his eternal power and divine nature, have been clearly perceived, ever since the creation of the world, in the things that have been made" (Rom. 1:20). And Scripture doesn't just *tell* us that creation communicates wisdom. It *shows* us. The Bible is rife with nature imagery, metaphors, and parables that draw truths out of the created world. Jesus himself constantly points his listeners to the wisdom of creation, whether to "consider the ravens" (Luke 12:24), or the lilies (Luke 12:27), or sheep, wolves, serpents, and doves (Matt. 10:16).

Again, the Bible is our primary and perfect source of communication from God. It is the most important book. But creation is a "second book." Augustine describes this "great book" by saying: "Look above you! Look below you! Note it. Read it. God, whom you want to discover, never wrote that book with ink. Instead He set before your eyes the things that He had made. Can you ask for a louder voice than that?"[6]

The "two books"—the special revelation of Scripture and the general revelation of nature—need not be in competition. We can, and should, affirm *sola Scriptura*, "but this principle does not forbid us from seeking knowledge of God from creation," writes John Frame, particularly because "the Bible itself speaks of natural revelation, and it presents that natural knowledge as a kind of prerequisite or prolegomenon to saving knowledge."[7]

Paul recognizes this when he preaches to pagans. Before he shares the specific gospel of Jesus Christ with them, he talks about the living God "who made the heaven and the earth and the sea and all that is in them," who "did not leave himself without witness, for he did good by giving you rains from heaven and fruitful seasons" (Acts 14:15, 17). At the Areopagus in Athens, Paul describes the "God who made the world and everything in it" (Acts 17:24), who created humans "that they should seek God, and perhaps feel their way toward him and find him" (v. 27). Paul begins here because he knows you can't live in this world, look at the sunsets, observe the genius of seasons and weather, without intuitively sensing a Creator.

God graciously *initiates* a conversation with us, revealing himself to us when he didn't have to. What a gift! He not only gives us a literal book we can read and preach; he gives us a book we can see, hear, smell, touch, and taste—a book that runs through our hands like warm sand, rushes over us like a cold mountain waterfall, trickles down our mouth like juice from a peach. All of it bears his mark.

Nature is one big, beautiful symphony that is always playing, if only we take out our earbuds long enough to listen.

What Creation Speaks about God

If we listen to the declarations of nature, what do we hear? If nature reveals truth because it reveals aspects of God, what are those aspects? One could write a whole book on just this question. For a start, consider this passage from Jonathan Edwards:

> The easiness and naturalness of trees and vines are shadows of His beauty and loveliness. The crystal rivers and murmuring streams are the footsteps of His favor, grace, and beauty. When we behold the light and brightness of the sun, the golden edges of an evening cloud, or the beauteous rainbow, we behold the adumbrations of His glory and goodness; and in the blue sky of His mildness and gentleness.[8]

There are so many ways nature reveals the glorious attributes of God. Even in the present fallen state of creation, which longs and groans for redemption (Rom. 8:19–23), we get foretastes of Isaiah's beautiful vision: "Holy, holy, holy is the LORD of hosts; the whole earth is full of his glory!" (Isa. 6:3). Reginald Heber puts his spin on it in the hymn "Holy, Holy, Holy": "All thy works shall praise thy name, in earth and sky and sea."[9] *All* thy works. The *whole* earth. From Mount Everest to Iguazu Falls, the Bayou swamps to the Siberian tundra, and every creek, valley, and plain in between: it's all "charged with the grandeur of God."[10]

The sheer diversity, and yet unity, of creation reveals something about the one-and-manyness of the triune God. The natural world is vast and complex, and yet everything is intricately fashioned and fit together. Psalm 104 is an epic celebration of the greatness of God revealed in the diversity of nature: water, wind, fire, mountains, valleys, springs, cedar trees, wild donkeys, rock badgers, lions, wild goats, the moon, the sun, and even a sea creature called "Leviathan." Verse 24 sums it up: "O LORD, how manifold are your works! In wisdom have you made them all; the earth is full of your creatures."

Creation also speaks to the *bigness* of God and gives us a healthy sense of perspective. Even non-religious people sense this when they stand before El Capitan in Yosemite or at the base of the Perito Moreno glacier in Patagonia. We feel this especially when we look up at the vast expanses of space. I remember lying on my back in a field as a kid at summer camp in Lake Geneva, Wisconsin, looking at the stars and feeling God's majestic bigness. How small am I! But I also marveled at the *love* of God—that this star-creating God also created me, to know him and feel his love as I lay in the soft, wet, Wisconsin grass.

This is a truth nature speaks: God is both glorious *and loving*. "Bound by no inner necessity or thirst for self-completion, the triune God created the wondrous speck of dust and water that we inhabit along with billions of galaxies for the sheer love of it—and of us," Michael Horton writes. "Love and glory become virtually indistinguishable as the motivation and final end of God's creative act. God's glory is his love, and his love is his glory."[11]

God's glorious love is revealed to us, in part, in the extravagant beauty of the created world. God didn't have to create over three hundred species of hummingbirds and thirty thousand species of orchids. He didn't have to create the cacao bean and sugar cane, and humans with the creative genius to make chocolate. But he did. What a gratuitously loving God! "The entire material universe speaks of God's love, his boundless affection for us," Pope Francis writes. "Soil, water, mountains: everything is, as it were, a caress of

God."[12] This "caress" is there to be felt, whether you're gardening in your backyard or strolling along a rocky coastline. It's the soothing comfort of a God who created this world for us to inhabit and cultivate, to know and be known within. It's "the peace of wild things," as Wendell Berry might say.[13]

To be sure, creation is not always a source of peace. We see its dark side in the devastation of hurricanes, earthquakes, famines, pandemics, and other calamities; we grieve the fallen creation when we attend a baby's funeral or watch a loved one deteriorate from cancer. We groan for restoration, for the new creation future where lions, lambs, wolves, leopards, cobras, and babies will coexist peacefully and the whole earth will be "full of the knowledge of the Lord" (Isa. 11:6–9). But even when nature is ugly, the beauty of God's power and the promise of renewal are on display. The charred ground of burnt forests creates nutrient-rich soil, ready for rebirth. The pruning of dead branches and shedding of dead leaves prepares the way for new buds of life. Throughout nature these cycles declare the glory of a death-conquering Savior who makes all things new.

The Sanity of Nature in an Insane World

Sadly, instead of availing ourselves of the wisdom, comfort, and sanity of God's "second book," many of us are spending more time in concrete jungles and screen-mediated virtual worlds. Naturally, it's making us crazy. The more we are disconnected from the design of God's world and out of sync with its natural rhythms, the more we are liable to not think of God much, or think *we* are god (by bending nature to our will), thus cutting ourselves off from our chief hope for wisdom and health. The urbanizing and digitizing of the world are accelerating the problem. We are becoming further removed "from the beating heart of things," as one writer put it, where "we experience more of life secondhand than first, scrolling through pictures of other people's experiences" and living from one abstraction to the next.[14]

In his book, *Last Child in the Woods*, Richard Louv coins the term "nature deficit disorder" and describes the negative mental, physical, and spiritual effects of the "de-naturing" of childhood. He decries the loss of "free-range play" for today's over-protected children, who increasingly spend more time on devices than they do exploring the wild outdoors. Yet nature, Louv writes, "offers something that the street or gated community or computer game cannot." It offers kids "an environment where they can easily contemplate infinity and eternity."[15]

In *The Nature Fix: Why Nature Makes Us Happier, Healthier, and More Creative*, Florence Williams cites studies that show urban living is literally changing our brains, increasing our odds of schizophrenia, anxiety, and mood disorders. Further, today's excess of digital stimuli causes our brains to become overwhelmed as they filter and sort through the glut. Being in nature, by contrast, gives us fewer choices, allowing the brain's attentional system to function better in higher order things like deep thinking and reflection. Two South Korean studies sent technology-addicted children on trips to forests and found that they came back with lowered cortisol levels and reported feeling happier and less anxious.[16] The empirical proof of nature's calming power is leading countries like Korea and Japan to designate "healing forests" where over-mediated digital ghosts can escape cities, go on a walk, breath oxygen, and recalibrate. The "forest therapy" trend is spreading in the United States as well, where some doctors are writing "nature prescriptions" and instructing patients to spend more time outdoors.[17]

Why does it work like this? Researchers are trying to figure it out using empirical methods, but the spiritual reality seems obvious:

we feel more at peace when we are in God's creation because that is what we are too: God's creation. When we feel our *createdness* more directly (as we do in nature, whether huffing and puffing in altitude or sweating in a humid field), we naturally feel closer to our Creator and thus happier. We are in our proper place.

Humans Are Part of Nature

One of the ways nature can become a source of *folly* rather than wisdom is when we elevate it to a higher plane than humanity. This is why some nature-loving people in today's world are decidedly *unwise*. They forget that nature includes *human* nature. We are God's creation too, and in a more profound sense than trees, streams, foxes, and fish. We are created in God's image (Gen. 1:27), a little lower than the angels and crowned with glory and honor (Ps. 8:5). This cannot be said of other creatures God made, or any "creature" *we* might make (e.g., robots and AI). Only humans bear God's image, and we are "fearfully and wonderfully made" (Ps. 139:14). Only humans have *conscience*—the imprint of God's moral wisdom. This conscience "will not stop speaking to us, accusing us," writes Frame. "Within us, it makes its case for God."[18] Is human conscience an infallible source of truth? No, because we are fallen and prone to suppress or distort it. We need Scripture to *train*, awaken, and sharpen our conscience. That's why the Bible comes first in the Wisdom Pyramid. Without it, listening to our conscience can become dangerously cloudy and subjective.

One of the implications of humans being not only *part* of nature, but the "crown" of it, is that it makes little sense to support protection for trees and whales but not humans. "It is clearly inconsistent to combat trafficking in endangered species while remaining completely indifferent to human trafficking, unconcerned about the poor, or undertaking to destroy another human being deemed unwanted," writes Pope Francis, who also notes that concern for the protection of nature is "incompatible with the justification of abortion."[19] This is logic even a progressive, pro-choice feminist like Camille Paglia has recognized. In a remarkable 2016 article on abortion, Paglia writes: "A liberal credo that is variously anti-war, anti-fur, vegan, and committed to environmental protection of endangered species like the sage grouse or spotted owl should not be so stridently withholding its imagination and compassion from the unborn."[20]

The Wisdom of the Body

Because humans are "fearfully and wonderfully made" by an ingenious craftsman (Ps. 139:14), it should be no surprise that our physical makeup itself manifests abundant truth. To be sure, the post-fall body's wisdom is imperfect—that's why various physical desires and anomalies should not be construed as "the way things were meant to be." Still, our given physical bodies, as fashioned by God, are astonishing reservoirs of truth if we only accept them as such.

There is wisdom, for one, in realizing what the body *can* do. With every new discovery in brain science we uncover new wonders about this most mysterious of organs. The more we know about DNA and genetics, the more humbled we should be at the miracle of our makeup. When my wife was pregnant, it blew my mind to watch her body's natural adjustments unfold. Various hormones were released that both provided physical needs (e.g., milk production) and emotional needs (stimulating nurturing instincts); her body's bone structure and physical proportions changed. As the due date neared, it was insane what the body did. And none of it happened because my wife *did anything* to make it happen. The body just knew and did what it needed to do to produce new life.

But there is also wisdom in realizing what the body *can't* do. It is God's gift that he made us with limitations. We need to sleep, for example. We need food and water to survive. We can't be in two places at once. Nature often gives us a healthy reminder of our fragility and smallness. An ocean current is stronger than we are; a lion's jaw is more powerful than we are; gravity is a thing. To be in nature is to be humbled, to hear the chastening voice of God to Job: "Where were you when I laid the foundation of the earth?" (Job 38:4). It is to know on a bodily, heart-pumping level that God is God, and we are not.

This is one of the most important lessons of nature—we are *creatures* and not the Creator. Our bodies, and the natural world, are not just playthings to manipulate and modify to suit our wills; they are gifts to accept, respect, and carefully steward. And yet this is a lesson lost on many today, who assume an autonomy that denies our creatureliness. It is the height of contradiction that vast segments of the pro-environment population—who rightly recognize the harm in genetically modified vegetables, inorganic chemical fertilizers, and so forth—are also advocates for the chemical and surgical manipulation that allow humans to "modify" their hormones and sexual organs. Surely if "organic" is best in strawberries and kale, it is also best in humans.

The givenness of nature should be welcomed and respected *across the board*, not just when it suits our politics. Again, even Paglia—as libertarian as she is on sexuality and gender—recognizes the inconsistency of progressives who appeal to biology on something like global warming but "flee all reference to biology when it comes to gender." She writes:

> The cold biological truth is that sex changes are impossible. Every single cell of the human body (except for blood) remains coded

with one's birth gender for life. Intersex ambiguities can occur, but they are developmental anomalies that represent a tiny proportion of all human births.[21]

Progressives fail to see that they cannot reject the body's organic givenness on sex and gender and then demand that everyone respect and protect the organic givenness of oceans, forests, and other ecosystems. Any genuine human ecology, Pope Francis writes, includes "learning to accept our body, to care for it and to respect its fullest meaning," which includes its femininity or masculinity.[22]

God created us sexually different, male and female (Gen. 1:27), for a reason. We see this when we look at our different bodies, when we recognize that only in their "different-ness" can new life be made. But the beauty of complementary pairs is also all around us in nature—day and night, ground and sky, land and sea—if we have eyes to see. Philosopher Peter Kreeft, for example, says this about the intersection of rock ("one of the most masculine things in the world") and sea ("one of the most feminine things in the world"):

> They're deeply satisfying together, and we can't quite analyze why we find that satisfaction and that peace and that sense of rightness. . . . The shore is the most popular place on earth. Waterfront property is the most expensive property anywhere in the world. Because that's where the sea and the land meet. That's where man and woman meet. The land without the sea is kind of boring, desert. The sea without the land is kind of boring. When are we going to land the ship? But the place where they meet, that's where all the action is. And that's where we want to be.[23]

On the biological level alone, male is no more interchangeable with female than water is interchangeable with rock or night interchangeable with day. Try as we might, humans will never be able to create new life without male plus female, just as a field of seeds will never sprout if only dust, not water, falls on the ground. The complementarity of gender isn't a menace or construct, but—like the coastlines and lakefronts and river trails we love—an irresistible source of beauty and life.[24]

The Folly of Denying and Destroying Creation

In America today, liberals call out conservatives for *destroying* creation. Conservatives call out liberals for *denying* creation. But the reality is *both* denying and destroying creation are utter folly.

Paul makes it clear in Romans 1:18–32 that it is folly to deny God's natural revelation in creation. "Claiming to be wise, they became fools" (v. 22), says Paul in reference to people who know God is real but do not honor him or give thanks to him (v. 21), exchanging the truth about God for a lie and worshiping the creature rather than the Creator (v. 25). It is significant that Paul's illustration of this is homosexual behavior, for few things show the rejection of God's created order more vividly than men or women "exchanging natural relations [with the opposite sex]" for same-sex relations that "are contrary to nature" (v. 26). This rejection of God's natural revelation is especially egregious because in rejecting God's male-female, "one flesh in marriage" design for sexuality, we are rejecting an aspect of God's creation that Paul says is a profound reflection of Christ's relationship to the church (Eph. 5:31–32).

Denying the good gift of creation is folly, but so is destroying it. To shrug at the pollution of God's natural creation, and the precious image-bearing humans within it, is to scoff at God and reject the beauty and wisdom of what he has made. Christians must see that our apathy about the degrading of creation contributes to the

Romans 1 style of moral confusion that arises when the truths that nature speaks are muffled or damaged. I agree with Gavin Ortlund when he says, "Christians should be the best environmentalists on the planet,"[25] in part because we know how much can go wrong when the symphony of creation is muted or silenced. I love how Tim Keller puts it, commenting on Psalm 19 ("the heavens declare . . ." v. 1):

> The Bible says creation is speaking to you. The stars. The waterfall. The animals, the trees. They have a voice. They are telling you about the glory of God. And it's your job as stewards of creation, as stewards of nature, to make sure they keep speaking, to not let that voice go out.[26]

It is folly to do anything—either intentionally or by neglect—that silences the voice of creation. To do so is to cut ourselves off from a key source of wisdom, but also a key context for worship. As Francis Schaeffer writes in *Pollution and the Death of Man*, "If I love the Lover, I love what the Lover has made."[27]

May we demonstrate our love for God by loving his creation, cherishing it, and learning from it—becoming wise as we accept with gratitude that every created thing gives glory to the Creator. May we join our voices with the stars, skies, fireflies, and everything else: "All creatures of our God and King, lift up your voice and with us sing . . . O praise Him!"[28]

DISCUSSION QUESTIONS

1. Think of a specific example where something you encountered or observed in nature illuminated an aspect of God or theology. How has the "handiwork" of God's creation helped you better understand the artist Creator?

2. In what ways does disconnection from nature—living more in our heads and on our computers than in the tangible, physical world—lead us to folly and confusion?

3. Science, as the study of nature, is important for the cultivation of wisdom. Why, then, are so many Christians skeptical about science? Why have science and faith often been pitted against one another?

Chapter 7

BOOKS

It is the glory of God to conceal things,
but the glory of kings is to search things out. PROVERBS 25:2

THE FOUNDATION FOR WISDOM is the book of books, the Bible. Another powerful source of wisdom, as we saw in the last chapter, is the "book" of nature—God's general revelation through his creation. These "two books" are important sources of truth because their author is God himself. All other books are man-made. However brilliant they are, they are imperfect, lesser sources of truth. But that doesn't make them unimportant.

On the contrary, books are vital in cultivating wisdom—not only for the truths they contain, but also for the way they help us *think*. In our distracted age, books give us perspective, focus, and space to reflect. Reading books—a wide variety, from different eras and places and worldviews, both fiction and nonfiction—keeps our anachronism and self-centeredness in check. They educate us, help us make connections across disciplines, and open up the world.

Other forms of culture do this too, of course—music, theater, cinema, the visual arts, poetry (see chapter 8). But the written word plays a special role in the passing on of wisdom. Words and books "allow for precision and nuance that images and music generally don't permit," writes literature professor Mark Edmundson. "Through words we represent ourselves to ourselves; we fix our awareness of who and what we are. Then we can step back and gain distance on what we've said. With that perspective comes the possibility for change."[1]

When I was a child, my dad would read books to me on his lap. When I learned to read on my own, he would often take me and my sister to the Broken Arrow, Oklahoma, public library, signing us up for summer reading programs and giving prize incentives for our reading progress. Trips to Mardel's, Waldenbooks, and other long-since-closed brick-and-mortar bookstores were common delights. We splurged on the Scholastic Book Fair. I had shelves of Hardy Boys books and the entire collection of Frank Peretti's Cooper Kids Adventure series (basically Indiana Jones for evangelical kids). Later I graduated to Goosebumps and John Grisham novels.

Were these particular books bastions of truth and wisdom for me? Probably not. But they instilled in me a love of reading that continues to this day (my current to-read stack is about twelve deep). Not every book I read is helpful; certainly not all are wise. But enough are. And the cumulative good of reading books is profound. Here are a few reasons why.

Books Help Us Connect

Books foster connection in at least two senses. They connect us with other people, and they connect the dots of ideas. They are massively important sources of both empathy and synthesis—two things vital for increasing wisdom, yet on the decline in today's frenetic age.

When we read books, we are stepping into another's shoes. We are entering the author's world, giving our attention to the author's perspective *for an extended time.* This last part is key. It's hard to develop empathy when you only read a tweet by someone; but a book-length immersion in someone's world creates the opportunity for *understanding.* The act of reading a book is literally the act of being "quick to listen, slow to speak." In literary fiction, we develop empathy by getting inside characters' minds. We may love or hate them, but to the extent that we listen to and live with them for a time, we can learn from the particularity of their existence. Research shows that literary fiction especially helps readers develop empathy—a better understanding of the complexity of what others are thinking and feeling.[2] Reading novels reminds us "that it's possible to connect with some[one] else even though they're very different from you," as Barack Obama said in an interview with Marilynne Robinson.[3] It's easy to dismiss one another's perspectives in a hyper-fast social media world. And so with every Graham Greene, Ernest Hemingway, or Toni Morrison character we meet, we recognize there are as many distinct human stories as there are stars in the sky, and each adds a particular gleam, color, and texture to our constellation of wisdom.

But books also help *make connections.* A constellation becomes a constellation, after all, only after you connect the dots to reveal some meaningful shape. One of the best feelings in reading a book, whether a novel or a memoir or an academic tome, is the moment of epiphany where a connection takes shape. *This* connects with *that!* Eventually the connecting puzzle pieces reveal a more intelligible image that helps us make sense of this crazy, complex world. As we read more books—and ideally a diverse array of books—our understanding of the world is simultaneously complicated and clarified. On one page we have lightbulb moments, making new sense of some things. Another page unravels what we thought we knew, raising new questions and sending us on new explorations. Such is the nature of *learning*. The more we read, the hungrier we are for more.

Books Are Windows and Doors

We read to connect, but also to explore. Even though we technically read a book without ever physically going anywhere, we all know the feeling of how a book transports us to other places and other times. I love that Christopher Nolan's sci-fi film *Interstellar* uses a bookshelf as a primary metaphor for communicating across the dimensions of space and time. Books are time machines, sending us back to the French Revolution or the American Civil War, Homer's Ithaka or Shakespeare's Verona. Books are the most efficient means of travel. In Mark Twain we can sail the Mississippi; in Rudyard Kipling we can explore the jungles of India. Before I physically visited the American South, I went there through the stories of Harper Lee, Flannery O'Connor, Eudora Welty, and others. We may never visit Nigeria or Colombia, but reading novels by Chinua Achebe or Gabriel García Márquez can bring aspects of those places to us.

In *An Experiment in Criticism*, C. S. Lewis talks about how each of us naturally only sees the world from one point of view, yet we want to "see with other eyes, to imagine with other imaginations, to feel with other hearts, as well as with our own."

> We demand windows. Literature as Logos is a series of windows, even of doors. One of the things we feel after reading a great work is 'I have got out.' Or from another point of view, 'I have got in;' pierced the shell of some other monad and discovered what it is like inside.[4]

Books broaden our horizons and correct our assumptions by showing us other contours of truth beyond our subjective experience ("rejecting the facts as they are for us in favour of the facts as they are," Lewis says).[5] They also help us escape loneliness. To read books is to enter a community. Writer Susan Sontag once described how, as a young girl, she would lie in bed and gaze at her bookcase, which was "like looking at my fifty friends."[6] Marilynne Robinson describes her collection of books in similar terms, as "my cloud of witnesses to the strangeness and brilliance of human experience, who have helped me to my deepest enjoyments of it."[7]

Books are open doors. Windows to the world. Wardrobes into Narnia. As a kid reading *Robinson Crusoe*, *The Cay*, *Island of the Blue Dolphins*, and *The Swiss Family Robinson*, it was delightful to imagine myself in these sea-swept, swashbuckling adventures in exotic and tropical locales (I was a landlocked Midwestern boy). I now see how these books enlarged my world, trained my imagination, and stoked curiosity in ways that have been indispensable to my intellectual and spiritual development. I am who I am today because of these ostensibly "escapist" childhood books. When we escape not to avoid reality but to encounter it, not to dull our senses but to enliven them, escapism is a good thing. And in today's stifling, self-absorbed, reality-denying world, books are among the best escape routes we have.

Books Help Us Think Well

There is a growing body of research that shows the powerful ways reading books—long, immersive reading in contrast to the fragmented, quick-scan reading we do online—strengthens our brains' abilities to think well. In her book, *Reader, Come Home: The Reading Brain in a Digital World*, Maryanne Wolf explores this research and argues that deep reading is a powerful booster shot for our brains at a time when they are increasingly weakened by digital overload.

"Those who have read widely and well will have many resources to apply to what they read," Wolf writes, while those who don't will have "less basis for inference, deduction, and analogical thought," making them "ripe for falling prey to unadjudicated information, whether fake news or complete fabrications."[8]

At a time when the glut, speed, and tailored-to-you nature of information is making us ever more prone to misinformation and unsound wisdom, reading books offers a powerful antidote. Books confront the "too much information" problem by focusing our attention on one thing for a longer, deeper time. They confront the "too fast" problem by forcing us to sit with one writer's perspective for long enough to really grapple with it. Books challenge the "too focused on me" problem by putting us in another's shoes.

Books give us solid grounding at a time when everything is up for grabs. They offer rubrics to better evaluate the barrage of information we face in today's world. In a world of snapshots and soundbites, books offer fuller context, and as Andy Crouch writes, "generally speaking, the older the book, the deeper the context."[9] Edmundson says people who read great works "will not be overly susceptible to the culture industry's latest wares. They'll be able to sample them, or turn completely away—they'll have better things on their minds."[10] This is because reading books—and education generally—trains our brains to better handle complex information, to reflect and evaluate rather than just accept. To read well is not to take everything the author says at face value. Rather, it is to understand the author's argument as best as we can, learn from it, but check it against what else we know. To read and learn well is to develop the ability to encounter a work in a nuanced way, filing away what's good and dismissing what's not.

But reading is not merely a defensive act. To read and learn well we must also be *teachable*, willing to let our guard down enough to be impressionable (but not gullible). When we open a book we should be ready to be changed, open to being convinced, eager to learn something we didn't know. If you think you know everything, you'll have no use for books; if you are humble and curious (key foundations for a life of wisdom), you'll devour them. It's not a co-incidence that the wisest people I know are not know-it-alls. What they know for sure is they *don't* know it all. They are eager to be taught, enlightened, influenced.

This is a key, yet countercultural, aspect of reading well. We live in a "death of expertise" world, after all (see chapter 3). Our prevailing hermeneutic is suspicion. We are more comfortable proclaiming ourselves experts than we are being swayed or influenced by others. That's why today's discourse is at an impasse. We've so emphasized "you do you" liberty that expert knowledge, educated consensus, and logic no longer matter. It's the problem educators face when they so emphasize students "learning to think for themselves" that the teacher's own credentials and authority to adjudicate right and wrong answers loses any force.

Reading books reminds us we are permeable creatures, by nature open to influence, and that this is how we grow. Every book we read reminds us reality isn't ours to make up as we like it. Reality includes us but is far bigger than we are. We don't create it as much as observe it. It's less something we write than something we read.

What Books Should You Read?

By now I hope you're convinced about the benefits of books for gaining wisdom. But what *sorts* of books should we read? If you're like me, the "information overload" problem extends to books too. There are way more "must-reads" than I could ever read. My nightstand stack is a precarious "Jenga meets Pisa" tower. Social media makes it worse because people whose taste I admire are always recommending books. Where do I start? What should I prioritize?

In one sense, to read *any* book is better than nothing. So go to a library (they still exist!) or a bookstore (if you can find one), and just explore. If something jumps out to you, read it! But what happens when your to-read list becomes overwhelmingly long? I have found myself so pressured by the size of my book stack that I end up speed-reading or scanning books mostly to just check them off. This is a terrible way to read. As with most things, quality is more important than quantity. Reading one great book slowly and deeply is better for our wisdom diet than reading five semi-insightful books at a breakneck pace. Be smarter about what you choose to read. Here are a few suggestions for how to make better selections.

1. READ OLD BOOKS

This is a good place to start. In most cases, classics are classics because they contain truth that has resonated across time and space. So much of what we read on the Internet (hot takes, Twitter threads, blog rants) will be forgotten within days. Many new-release books will similarly fade quickly. But the old books, the "great books," have lasted because their wisdom is durable in a transitory world. Given the choice between something on the current bestseller list or something on a "greatest books of all time" list, go with the latter.

In his preface to Athanasius's *On the Incarnation* (a very great, old book!), C. S. Lewis wisely observes that a new book "is still on its trial" and must be "tested against the great body of Christian thought down the ages." He suggests a rule I have tried to follow: read one old book for every three new books. Lewis explains the reasoning:

Every age has its own outlook. It is specially good at seeing certain truths and specially liable to make certain mistakes. We all, therefore, need the books that will correct the characteristic mistakes of our own period. And that means the old books.[11]

Far from stale relics, old books are often the *most* relevant to our present. They have enough distance to speak boldly and clearly to our situation, without the blind spots and inflections of bias that inhibit our judgment. "A given age is likely to be infused to the core with standard prevailing opinion," Edmundson argues. "One way to break through that prevailing opinion is to have recourse to the best that has been known and thought in the past."[12]

2. READ BOOKS THAT CHALLENGE YOU

Another priority for a healthy reading diet is to choose books that will challenge you. Read outside your comfort zone. Read fiction when you prefer nonfiction. Read a diverse array of genres. Read books by people whose lives and perspectives are different from yours. Christians should read books written by non-Christians. Democrats should read books written by Republicans, and vice versa. It's tempting to mostly read books by people who share your perspective. I certainly struggle with this, because it's hard to read books that make me angry on almost every page. But I know it can reap great rewards in cultivating wisdom.

Here's a radical thought for today's echo chamber world: you can benefit from reading something even if you disagree with much of it! An educated mind can entertain and grapple with another's ideas without accepting them. Christians have often been guilty of sheltering our young from books, movies, and other narratives that might propagate "dangerous" ideas. But this can backfire. Instead we should teach young people to read both humbly and critically, with open but discerning minds.

3. READ BOOKS YOU ENJOY

Don't just read old and challenging books. Read things that give you pleasure! As Alan Jacobs notes in his wonderful book, *The Pleasures of Reading in an Age of Distraction*, don't turn reading into "the intellectual equivalent of eating organic greens." Instead, "read what gives you delight—at least most of the time—and do so without shame." A steady diet of only great books would be like eating at the most elegant restaurants every day, argues Jacobs. "It would be too much."[13]

Read things that stoke your love of reading. If you've been slogging through a book for eight months and can hardly muster energy to turn the page, don't force yourself to continue! Move on to something more enjoyable. And if you love a book, revisit it! Feel no shame in re-reading your favorite books rather than reading that new buzz-worthy bestseller. There are countless Pulitzer Prize-winning novels I have not yet read, but I still find time to re-read *The Great Gatsby* every couple of years (usually in April). Reading what we love keeps us loving reading.

Great Books and the Greatest Book

Some Christians might question the value of reading "secular" books. If God is the ultimate source of infallible truth, how much wisdom can we glean from writers who don't know him? Why read books by atheists when I could read books by people whose souls are enlightened by the Holy Spirit? Fair questions.

But if God created the world, and if he is the source and standard of truth, then all truth is his. If we believe everything in creation bears the mark of the Creator, then any book—whether philosophy, biography, biology, or fiction—that puts this creation under the microscope has potential to illuminate truth. "All branches of heathen learning have not only false and superstitious fancies," Augustine wrote, "but they contain also liberal instruction which is better adapted to the use of the truth, and some most excellent precepts of morality; and some truths in regard even to the worship of the One God are found among them."[14] We can thus read a "heathen" book with a Christian lens, discarding its falsehoods and mining its truths.

Still, we must put these books in their proper place. It would be folly to build one's wisdom diet around great books but not also the greatest book, the Bible. Without the reference point of God, the "truth" of books is relative. One reader might find a book true, while another finds it false. There can be no consensus on canon if there is no transcendent reference point for words like *good, true*, and *beautiful*. "The only guarantor of communal truth is transcendent truth," writes David Lyle Jeffrey. "Without intellectually accountable access to the Greater Book, very many lesser, yet still very great, expressions of truth may go without understanding."[15]

Books are valuable sources for gaining wisdom, to be sure. But like every other category in the Wisdom Pyramid, they are valuable only insofar as they supplement God's word rather than replace it. They have the ability to make us wise as long as their assertions of truth are consistent with and not contrary to God's revealed truth. They are great books to the extent that they confirm and clarify the truth of the greatest book.

DISCUSSION QUESTIONS

1. Beyond the *content* of what we read in books, why is the *posture* of reading books conducive to gaining wisdom?

2. Why is it valuable to read books that challenge you or that contain ideas with which you strongly disagree?

3. How do you choose the books you read? How might you be more intentional about selecting books that are conducive to gaining wisdom?

Chapter 8

BEAUTY

Out of Zion, the perfection of beauty,
God shines forth. PSALM 50:2

A FEW YEARS AGO I had an experience of beauty I'll never forget—
in a cemetery. It was an Explosions in the Sky concert in the iconic
Hollywood Forever Cemetery. As I lay on a blanket in the grass, on a
cool May night, listening to the cacophonous instrumental music of
the Texas band (famous for their soundtrack to *Friday Night Lights*),
I remember feeling one of those gut-level brushes with eternity that
beauty uniquely provides. As I watched the tall palm trees swaying
in the cool wind, I imagined them as arms lifted in praise. As I lay
breathing, alive, on ground where hundreds of dead lie buried, I felt
the soaring guitars in songs like "Greet Death" and "The Birth and
Death of the Day" as declarations of resurrection: wordless testimo-
nies to hope for renewal, emptied graves, life after death.

How does beauty do this? It's mostly a mystery. It's impossible to
create theorems and testable hypotheses about what beauty is, how
it works, and why humans, throughout time, gravitate to it. But we
all know beauty exists. We know it when we see it, hear it, smell it,

taste it, touch it. It stirs our souls, wakes us up, and tunes our hearts to something harmonious and pleasant about the world. What is that something? I believe it is God. I believe all that is beautiful bears witness to God because God is the source and standard of beauty. As Jonathan Edwards put it, "All the beauty to be found throughout the whole creation, is but the reflection of the diffused beams of the Being who hath an infinite fullness of brightness and glory."[1]

In its very nature—superfluous, unnecessary, abundant—beauty teaches us about our abundant God, whose love and grace are bountiful in ways that a Mozart piano concerto or a Monet water lily can uniquely convey. Beauty shapes our hearts, orients our loves, quiets our minds, and stills our souls in a noisy and weary world. It's a profoundly important part of any wisdom diet.

Head and Heart

Wisdom is more than just what we know in our heads; it also involves our bodies, senses, emotions. Beauty works on these levels. It engages and stirs our hearts. It reveals truth on the *affective*, often subconscious level. It forms our *loves*. That's why movies, TV, and other narrative arts are so powerful in shaping popular opinions. They grab our hearts and move us viscerally, sometimes more powerfully than logic or reason. It's why music affects us in ways we can't fully explain. I listened to an instrumental song by Icelandic band Sigur Rós the other day and was instantly transported to a very specific moment, 18 years ago, when I listened to the same album on my iPod while riding the Metra in Chicago. In a mysterious way, music comes as close as anything to transcending time. Like other forms of beauty, music can help us *feel* something like eternity in ways the mind struggles to grasp.

Beauty gives truth a feeling, tone, and resonance. Truth without beauty often falls on deaf ears, just as beauty without truth rings hollow. But truth and beauty together are powerful, and we see this even in the Bible itself. God uses beauty to communicate in Scripture: story, metaphor, poetry, song, heroes and villains, and all manner of literary devices. Rather than speaking propositionally, as if his listeners were robots merely needing binary code, Jesus speaks cryptically, through parables that paint dramatic pictures and use memorable metaphors. By communicating to his creatures in a way that emphasizes the power of form, our Creator makes the best case for why beauty matters. Literature professor David Lyle Jeffrey puts it this way:

> In our own culture's terms, God does not talk like a lawyer, a philosopher, or even a theologian, let alone a TV talk-show host. Very often, however, he speaks like a poet. . . . The fact that God speaks poetry when the issues are most weighty suggests that appreciating his poetry might be an essential element in our knowledge of God; that is, we should understand him as a poet—the original Poet—the One who writes the world.[2]

Is beauty by itself sufficient for our knowledge of God? Of course not. There are plenty of artists and art lovers who love beauty, but who are somehow apathetic about God, beauty's source. Beauty and art provide wisdom only insofar as they are in some relationship or conversation with the Creator. Art is "a handmaiden to faith," Jeffrey writes. "Great art can give us a glimpse, when referred to its source, of the deep echo in beauty, especially in the beauty of a holy love, of the beauty of holiness, and thus of the love of our heavenly Father."[3]

Created in the Creator's Image

One reason why human creativity bears unique witness to God is that creativity is a key part of what it means to bear the image of

God. Horses did not paint the Sistine Chapel ceiling. Cows did not create the skyscraper or the smartphone. Humans did. Your pet dog may be cute, but it cannot write you a poem or create a Valentine's Day card for you. Your human child can.

In *The Mind of the Maker*, Dorothy Sayers ponders how, in the Genesis verses leading up to the "image of God" moment of Genesis 1:27, the only information we know about God is that he is a creator. "We find only the single assertion, 'God created,'" she writes. "The characteristic common to God and man is apparently that: the desire and the ability to make things."[4] We could say there is more to the *imago Dei* than our creative capacity, but there is certainly not less.

It's remarkable that humans can take the world they are born into—the "raw materials" of God's creation—and make something new of it, both in the sense of physically making and in *making sense* of it. When I look at the architecture of La Sagrada Família in Barcelona or the Burj Khalifa in Dubai, I cannot help but praise God for the glory of human ingenuity. When I drink coffee (blessed thing!) I cannot help but praise God for creating creatures in his image, with the capacity to dream up such a magisterial beverage through the bizarre process of roasting beans, grinding them, and filtering hot water through them. What a marvel!

We might say that every creative work is simply a remix of God's original masterwork. Van Gogh's *Starry Night* can only exist because God first created stars and the colors of night. Bach's "Cello Suite" can only exist because God created trees, whose wood is used to carve a cello, and horses, whose hair is used to fashion a bow. Beauty is beautiful because it demonstrates man's creative capacity to make new things out of the raw materials God provides. The Christian poet Richard Wilbur puts it this way:

In the strict sense, of course
We invent nothing, merely bearing witness
To what each morning brings again to light.[5]

Bearing Witness

The artist bears witness to what God has made. Beauty shines a spotlight on creation, focusing our attention on what we are often too busy or too distracted to see. Beauty heightens our senses and helps us *notice* the wonder around us—which is why beauty is more important than ever. Our over-mediated age is rife with visual stimuli. We glance at, scroll through, and passively watch all manner of things. But we increasingly don't have eyes to see reality. Due to what he calls the abundance of "visual noise" in today's world, Josef Pieper observes that "the average person of our time loses the ability to see because *there is too much to see!*"[6]

Our deep spiritual grief in the modern world is in part a result of this blindness. We fill our senses with all manner of diversion and distraction, constantly consuming whatever micro-spectacle comes across our feed. But we rarely stop long enough to appreciate, understand, or critically evaluate any of it. Artists help focus our attention and awaken our senses. The painter or photographer literally frames one rectangle view of reality so we can *see* something (whether a landscape, still life, or portrait) in a more concentrated way. The filmmaker captures time and space in a way that forces us to truly notice and contemplate both (if we're willing to put away our phones in the theater!).

Beauty can be a healthy part of one's wisdom diet, but only if it is in its proper place, as neither the most or least important "food group." When beauty occupies the preeminent place it can become an idol, a drug-like high we constantly chase. When beauty has *no* place in our diet, we miss out on certain textures, depths, and dynamics of truth. But in its right place, beauty can do wonders for our wisdom, helping us know and love God more by tasting, seeing, touching, smelling, and hearing his glories in the diverse harmony of creation.

Contrast and Tension

What makes something beautiful? There are many answers to that question, which is why the question of beauty is often assumed to be hopelessly subjective. But one thing most people can agree on is that a key attribute of beauty is *contrast*. Music is beautiful if it contains both soft and loud sections, pianissimo and fortissimo. Photographs are beautiful if there is contrast in color, light and dark. Films, novels, and plays are beautiful if they contain both heroes and villains, triumph and tragedy. A cookie is beautiful if it contains contrast in flavor (salty and sweet) and texture (crunchy and chewy).

Contrast is crucial to beauty: the juxtaposition, interplay, or coming together of different (often opposite) things. When daylight meets night, for example, we have sunsets or sunrises: the most beautiful and oft photographed times of day. When salt water meets fresh, we have estuaries: some of the most vibrant natural habitats in the world. When two different things come together, their seeming contrast often feels strangely coherent, creating beauty and life.

We register contrast as beauty because this is how God set up the world. In Genesis 1 we see how God created the world through a series of pairs: light and dark, evening and morning, waters above and below, land and sea, and finally, male and female. The beautiful contrast of man and woman is God's masterstroke, such that their "one flesh" union in marriage is said to be an earthly pointer to the heavenly reality of how Jesus loves his church (Eph. 5:31–32). That marriage is, in a mysterious way, the epitome of God-given beauty, is reinforced by the fact that it bookends the Bible. God's story begins with a wedding in Eden and ends with one in Revelation, a book full of contrasting pairs: Christ and his bride (the church), heaven and earth, and the climactic clash of good and evil.

This contrast of good and evil may not seem beautiful on the surface, but it speaks to another fundamental element of beauty, closely related to contrast: tension. The most beautiful things in life contain a felt dissonance that points to a longed-for resolution. A symphony is beautiful when it contains unresolved chords that point to an elusive aural "home" (which usually comes in the final movement). A play is beautiful when its protagonist faces setback after setback, only to reach a cathartic resolution in the end. The arc of almost every compelling story follows a familiar, tension-filled structure: paradise, paradise lost, paradise restored.

The beautiful tension in art reminds us of the beautiful tension in existence: our hopeless plight met with divine rescue; our struggle with sin met with the sinless Savior who defeated death. It's the tension of the "already, not-yet" kingdom of God. We live in the Saturday between the pain of Good Friday and the triumph of Easter Sunday. We celebrate and take comfort in the first advent of Christ—that he came and conquered sin and death on our behalf. But we wait and long for his second advent—when he will come on a white horse, his eyes ablaze and a sword coming out of his mouth (Rev. 19:11–16), to once and for all bring justice and resolution to this deeply broken world.

We live in the "meantime" space where tension reigns. We suffer, but with hope. We grow, but often in a "two steps forward, one step back" sort of way. We experience the tension Paul describes in Romans 7 and Romans 8—between slavery to sin ("I do the very thing I hate," 7:15) and Spirit-empowered freedom ("more than conquerors,"

8:37). Insofar as beauty helps make us more *aware* of this tension, it helps make us wise. Beauty is a window through which we see the world and God's glory within it; but it is also a mirror that helps us better see ourselves—our sinful plight, our need for redemption, our longing for peace.

Beauty Silences Us

I love the moment right at the end of some beautiful display, when the audience is—for a brief moment—dumbstruck and silent. In a movie, it's when the screen goes dark and the credits start to roll, and you sit with your thoughts in the theater (unless you need to run to the bathroom), pondering what you witnessed. In a concert, it's that moment after an epic song reaches its finale and the music stops, its glorious final notes echoing in your ears and soul. Wagner's *Das Rheingold* prelude, for example, builds and builds, with escalating string arpeggios and swells of cacophonous sound, and then it suddenly stops. The abrupt silence that follows the music is almost the most beautiful thing about it.

Beauty renders us mute. Oh how we need this in our noisy age! When we encounter something beautiful our first instinct should not be to take a selfie with it. Rather, we should be still, quiet, and amazed. Beauty can easily become noise when we encounter it only in that "constant barrage" sort of way, with quick glances and half-attention in the "in between" moments of life: an episode of a Netflix show while we make dinner; a few Spotify songs while we run on the treadmill; ten pages of a novel on Kindle as we wait to board an airplane. In today's over-mediated age it's possible to fill every spare moment with little flashes of beauty, but this only serves to eradicate the crucial component for gaining *wisdom* from the beauty we encounter—silence.

We are suffering from what Cal Newport calls "solitude deprivation": "A state in which you spend close to zero time alone with your own thoughts and free from input from other minds."[7] Matthew Crawford compares silence (or the absence of noise) to air and water, resources we take for granted that we need to survive: "Just as clean air makes respiration possible, silence . . . is what makes it possible to *think*."[8] But silence is a scarce resource in today's loud world.

We need to be intentional about cultivating spaces of silence and reflection, where our attention can be directed to one or two things rather than fifty. Making space for beauty is one way we fight against the solitude deprivation and desensitizing noise of our age. But to do this we need to also value things like rest and leisure, recognizing the importance of *unproductive* space and simply *being* in a world prone to filling every moment with *doing*. In his book *Leisure: The Basis of Culture*, Josef Pieper says leisure is "a form of silence" which is "the prerequisite of the apprehension of reality: only the silent hear and those who do not remain silent do not hear."[9] Silence and beauty go together. We need silence to fully experience beauty, and beauty helps foster in us silence. Beauty cultivates in us a calm serenity that makes Psalm 46:10 more real in our lives: "Be still, and know that I am God."

Beauty Helps Us Rest

Beauty quiets us in a noisy world, but it also helps slow us down. When humans work they reflect the image of a God who works. But we also image God when we rest, because God is a God who rests (Gen. 2:2–3). "The essence of being in God's image is our ability, like God, to stop," writes Peter Scazzero. "We imitate God by stopping our work and resting." And yet this is countercultural in a digital world where every moment can be optimized for productivity. The biblical notion of Sabbath challenges this mindset because it calls us to "build the doing of nothing into our schedules each week. . . . By the world's standards it is inefficient, unproductive, and useless."[10]

Beauty and Sabbath go hand in hand. Both are extravagant. Unproductive. Unnecessary. Both are reflections of God's abundance and reminders that the world is chiefly a gift to receive, not a prize to be earned. Beauty doesn't have to exist. The fact that humans delight in sunsets, symphonies, and well-proportioned faces has no bearing on our survival as a species. Mankind's pleasure in poetry and pecan pie cannot be explained by the Darwinian account of human existence. The only explanation that makes sense of beauty is that we are created in the image of God who relishes it; a non-utilitarian God. Just look at the ten thousand species of birds in the world, or the four hundred thousand species of flowers; each unique in color, shape, and texture. Consider the diversity of spices—from cumin to cayenne to nutmeg and turmeric. God could have created the world so that humans only needed to eat a bland, gruel-like substance in order to survive, but he didn't. He created thousands of edible plants and animals, from which millions of culinary combinations could be made. He created humans with taste buds to appreciate things like salted caramel gelato, buttermilk fried chicken, and lamb tagine. Just as he is a God who not only creates but pauses to *enjoy* what he has created (Gen. 1:31), so he created us with the capacity to *enjoy*. That's why beauty exists.

When we refuse to observe the Sabbath and don't allow space for the enjoyment of beauty, we implicitly signal a scarcity mentality that doubts the goodness of God. But when we do stop to rest, to feast, to "smell the roses" as they say, we display a contentedness and calm acceptance about the world and the one who holds it together—a confidence that however tragic and unpredictable it is, we can still pause for a party (or a nap). Pieper wisely compares the ability to enjoy leisure with the ability to sleep: "A man at leisure is not unlike a man asleep," he writes. "When we really let our minds rest contemplatively on a rose in bud, on a child at play, on a divine mystery, we are rested and quickened as though by a dreamless sleep."[11]

Beauty and Worship

As I've noted in various ways throughout this book, wisdom is not just *knowing* the right things. It's also (and largely) about having the right posture; having our loves rightly ordered. It's about recognizing that God doesn't want to just be known *about*. He wants to be loved. He wants us to experience his presence not just cerebrally but tangibly: in our bodies, our senses, our emotions.

This is why beauty has always been central in the worship practices of the church. We could just state propositions about God on Sundays. But we choose to sing them. We praise God through music, poetic liturgy, church architecture, and other forms of beauty. We emphasize physical rituals like baptism and the Lord's Supper because we recognize the importance of embodied *forms* in the shaping of our hearts: helping us not only to *know* Jesus, but also to *love* him, to feel him in our bones, to remember him *physically* as we take and eat the bread and drink the wine of communion.

The Lord's Supper encapsulates the sort of wisdom we find in beauty. It's an example of how a beautiful *form* can powerfully communicate an important truth. It's the gospel *enacted* by means of culture. We don't just eat raw grains and grapes in communion. We eat bread and wine—cultural products. It's a beauty that focuses us, demands our attention, silences us. There are few moments in modern life where multitudes of people are silent together, focused intently on one thing. But the Lord's Supper is one such moment, with every heart and mind contemplating the meaning of the bread and wine (or grape juice). Communion also beautifully manifests contrast (the elements are savory and sweet, solid and liquid), as well as tension: the Lord's Supper is an "already, not yet" ritual that both *remembers* the cross and *looks forward to* the heavenly feast to come. Finally, the Lord's Supper is beautiful in how it invites us to rest. When we come to the communion table on Sundays, bearing the immense burdens of the week, we say yes to Christ's invitation in Matthew 11:28: "Come to me, all who labor and are heavy laden, and I will give you rest." We acknowledge that he is enough: our bread, water, life, peace. No book, article, or tweet reminds us of the nourishing, saving grace of Jesus quite like the beauty of communion can.

And that's why beauty matters.

DISCUSSION QUESTIONS

1. We often think about wisdom in terms of the rational—knowledge and information that fill our brains. But what role do the heart and emotion play in wisdom, and how does beauty shape these parts of us?

2. How are beauty and Sabbath related? Why are things like rest, stillness, space, and quietness important for living a wise life?

3. Does an objective standard of beauty exist, or is beauty simply in the eye of the beholder? How might other sections of the Wisdom Pyramid help us answer this question?

Chapter 9

THE INTERNET AND SOCIAL MEDIA

Know this, my beloved brothers: let every person be quick to hear, slow to speak, slow to anger; for the anger of man does not produce the righteousness of God. JAMES 1:19-20

WE HAVE MADE IT to the top of the pyramid. But "top" in this case does not mean best. Like the "fats, oils, and sweets" food group atop the Food Pyramid, the Internet and social media should be a "use sparingly" portion of our wisdom diet.

The problem is we don't use the Internet and social media sparingly. We gorge on it like a Las Vegas all-you-can-eat buffet. We keep going back for more, and it's making us sick. But this does not mean there is *nothing* good to be found online. An all-you-can-eat buffet doesn't have to always make us sick, after all. With self-control and the right intentions, one can find healthy, delicious offerings in almost any buffet, or at least limit one's intake of the unhealthy things.

That's why the Internet and social media are still part of the Wisdom Pyramid. There *are* diamonds in the digital rough. And even if we wanted to rid our lives of the Internet and social media, could we?

For better or worse, smartphones have become our third arm—such that when we lose or can't find it, we feel like an amputee. Wi-Fi is our oxygen. To be somewhere in the world without it is to feel stifled, suffocated, cut off from life. These may be disturbing realities, but they are realities.

Sure, one could respond by living a totally analog, off-the-grid life—and maybe one would be happier for it. But what about everyone else? Many people today don't have the luxury of living offline. "Digital detoxes" are largely an activity of the privileged. We don't need extreme, either/or solutions for how to respond to the dangers of the Internet and social media. We do need models for how to navigate the Internet and social media carefully. We need habits that help us take what is good and avoid what is bad, habits conducive to gaining wisdom.

Three Ways the Internet and Social Media Benefit Wisdom

In what sense are the Internet and social media potentially valuable for wisdom? We know the many downsides to online life. What are the upsides? In my view there are at least three.

1. ACCESS

The Internet has removed barriers to accessing knowledge and education. If the idea of a public library (free access to books) was one small step in the direction of democratizing knowledge, the Internet was a giant leap. Today, if you have Internet access on your phone or computer, you have history's most potent library card. You have access to all the wise sages of the past—from Plato to Proust to Plantinga. On YouTube you can gain the knowledge you would get at a university. An uneducated pastor in rural India who might never be able to attend seminary can, through the Internet, access all manner of theological resources—essays, sermons, book reviews, video lectures—to help him better handle Scripture and care for his flock.

This is one of the reasons I love my job as an editor for The Gospel Coalition. We are a ministry made possible by the Internet, and our free theological resources reach Christians all over the world. It warms my heart to think of the new believer in Thailand who stumbles across a sermon from John Piper and gains a more robust theology of suffering, or the student in Madrid who reads something online by Tim Keller and gains new tools for engaging her secular neighbors. It's a joy to receive emails from pastors in Denmark or aspiring writers in Texas who are encouraged by the cultural analysis I write.

All this is made possible by the Internet. It's liberating for people to hear voices and perspectives they would not otherwise get in their home contexts. It's empowering to discover new models for how we might think and who we might become. The Internet can give us the reassurance of "you too?" It can introduce us to leaders, thinkers, and kindred spirits who give us the courage we wouldn't otherwise have had without their example. There are people I have never met in person but who have deeply shaped my life by what I've encountered of them online—whether through a blog or a podcast or an Instagram account.

The power of being influenced by what we find online has its downsides, of course—online voices can poison our souls as quickly as they can nourish them. But this just makes it all the more important to not abandon the Internet but rather seek to redeem it—amplifying the voices of truth and showcasing the exemplars of wisdom.

2. PLATFORM

If Internet *access* levels the playing field in terms of being *exposed* to more potential voices of truth, the *platform* power of the Internet levels the playing field in terms of giving *exposure* to worthy voices who might otherwise never be heard. Though it's easier said than done in today's noisy online world, in theory anyone with Internet access can create a social media account and *be heard*. You can lack money, connections, education, and similar privileges and still say or create something that, potentially, large numbers of people benefit from around the world. Whether you're an aspiring singer-songwriter, photographer, or simply someone with a story, you don't need a gatekeeper or publishing deal to get heard. You have direct access to your audience. But this is also the biggest challenge: How do you build an audience and get them to notice you in a world where people are exhausted by the volume of things already vying for their attention?

Still, the *potential* of platform is there. The Internet makes it possible for an unpublished writer to get a book deal because of a blog post that goes viral; for a kid with a creative YouTube channel to be hired by Disney; for a teenager with an Instagram account to become an "influencer" of millions. To be sure, more people with bigger audiences doesn't necessarily make the world a wiser place. But it does diversify the spectrum of voices out there. In the Internet age, historically marginalized or underrepresented voices can be widely heard. Social media is particularly powerful in this regard. At its best (and admittedly, it is rarely at its best), social media can be a village green where people can interact, debate, and learn from one another in ways they didn't before. Social media can be a spotlight that exposes corruption and raises awareness about oft-hidden struggles. It can be a cry for help for vulnerable people who won't get a hearing at home but find one on Twitter. It can be a testing ground where one's ideas are refined by feedback. It can be a confessional space for people struggling with all manner of things.

Does the ubiquity of platform—the fact that everyone now has a megaphone for amplifying their own voices—also add to the noise and confusion of our age? Certainly. But it can also introduce voices the world needs to hear.

3. CONSENSUS

One of the downsides of platform is the resulting noise of too many people publishing too many things. Thankfully, the Internet has a built-in mechanism that helps make the noise more manageable: consensus. This is the crowd-sourcing collective wisdom of Wikipedia, Amazon reviews, Yelp rankings, and YouTube "likes." What do we give our attention to in the age of information overload? The question would be a whole lot more debilitating if we didn't have the evaluative markers of the "like," the "share," the "retweet," and so on. The compounding power of "viral"—for all its problems—is at least a filter of sorts. If enough people start paying attention to and sharing something online, maybe it's worth our time?

Of course there are downsides to the viral effect too. The "pile on" effect, Twitter mobs, bandwagons, social contagions, "cancel culture," and rapidly disseminated falsehoods are all problematic results of the speedy gathering of online momentum. But at its best, this power can be harnessed to positive ends: bringing attention to unseen injustices, keeping powerful figures accountable, empowering people to break their silence and tell stories that need to be heard. The #MeToo movement is a good example of this. Through the power of social media and the "strength in numbers" safety it provided, many victims of abuse—who previously felt alone and feared speaking out—started sharing their stories online. As a result, much darkness was brought to light. Hard realities were made known. In many cases, sexual abusers were brought to justice.

The consensus power of the Internet can be a powerful check and balance. The critical importance of online reviews for things like hotels and restaurants keeps them accountable to having clean sheets, sanitary bathrooms, and tasty food. The consensus of Rotten Tomatoes can help a moviegoer choose a good movie or avoid a bad one. If a politician misspeaks or a reporter utters a falsehood, you can be sure the online masses won't let it slide. Very little can be hidden in the age of the Internet. Lies will inevitably be exposed. Misbehavior will be found out. Truth can emerge. If this somewhat scary reality keeps all of us on our toes a bit more, forcing a more careful and virtuous way of speaking and living, we should be grateful.

Five Habits for Cultivating Wisdom Online

The Internet and social media can help us become wise, but only if we approach them with great care and intention. To that end, here are five habits to consider as you evaluate the place of online media in your life.[1]

1. GO WITH A PURPOSE. DON'T JUST "SURF"!

"Surfing the Net" was one of the early metaphors for what we do online, bringing to mind a sort of leisurely, "we'll see where these links take me!" approach to riding the Web's waves. But it is precisely this posture—going online just to stroll (or should I say "scroll"?) around its wide-open spaces—that leads us to fill every spare moment of our lives with insipid social media debates, mildly amusing cat videos, and other online ephemera. It is precisely this unconscious impulse to hop on our phone and just go *somewhere* that can lead us to dark places: pornography, toxic subcultures, fruitless comment section battles. Sadly, the ease with which we can jump online in our spare moments (whether 30 seconds at a stop light or 90 seconds in the Chick-fil-A drive-thru line) conditions us to eliminate every last shred of unmediated space in our lives—which is a terrible thing for cultivating wisdom.

In his helpful book *The Common Rule*, Justin Earley suggests our spare moments should not be filled with online wandering, but rather "reserved for staring at walls, which is infinitely more useful." He also suggests avoiding social media in bed and avoiding unplanned scrolling, which "usually means I'm hungry for something to catch my eye—and plenty of strange, dark, and bizarre things are happy to catch the eye on social media."[2] The digital wanderer is asking for trouble. Don't go online without a plan. Go with a purpose, and stay online only as long as you need to.

2. QUALITY OVER QUANTITY

Given the glut of options online, and the above point that your online time should be limited only to purposeful activities rather than aimless wandering, it's important to make the time matter. Consider following Cal Newport's advice in *Digital Minimalism*, which he defines as "a philosophy of technology use in which you focus your online time on a small number of carefully selected and optimized activities that strongly support things you value, and then happily miss out on everything else."[3]

How does one carefully select what to read, watch, listen to, or experience online? First, listen to the recommendations of trusted people in your life. Given the choice between reading an article that just popped into your Twitter feed because an advertiser put it there or reading an article because ten people you trust shared it on Facebook, go with the latter. Check out reviews of books from trusted websites before you decide what to read. Consult the writing of trusted film critics before choosing what to watch. Limit yourself to one podcast or one Netflix show a month, and only the ones enough trustworthy people have recommended. In a world where your time is scarce and everything is vying for your attention, don't be a passive consumer who clicks on whatever comes your way. Be happy to bypass most of it, trusting that a smaller amount of excellent, curated dishes will be better for your wisdom diet than a vast amount of hit-or-miss, haphazard snacks.

3. SLOW DOWN!

Even if you can't control the speed of things online, you can control *your* speed. And a slower pace is almost always more conducive to wisdom. One of this book's recurring themes is the notion that time is a great filter for wisdom: the longer something lasts, the likelier it is to contain value. Don't spend your time reading the hottest take or the "trending now" video. Instead, wait a bit and read the (usually better) cold takes. Read the *Atlantic* article from five years ago that people still reference; watch the "classics" of YouTube before the flavor-of-the-week clip. Once the novelty of something wears off, if people are *still* recommending it, maybe it's actually worth your time. Don't fear missing out on most things online. Most of it is missable and will be quickly forgotten. To slow down—until history's filter gives you reason to pay attention—is to be a wiser consumer online.

The same goes for what you *contribute* online. Speed is treacherous when it comes to posting your opinion on social media or fanning some rapidly spreading flame. We often jump on an online bandwagon before we realize it has a broken axle. Take time to vet the truth and consider the wisdom of something before you share it, to consider the potential impact of your words before you post. Remember Scripture's "slow to speak" wisdom.

4. DIVERSIFY YOUR EXPOSURE

As digital media becomes ever more tailored to individual consumers and their algorithm-perfected preferences, the problems explored in chapter 3 are only exacerbated. But we can combat this by being intentional about diversifying the voices we listen to. Don't just read articles from the same bias-confirming sources. Don't only tune in to the radio shows where your opinions are confirmed. Challenge yourself by actually giving attention to well-articulated versions of the "other side" of arguments. Respect your ideological opponent (and yourself!) by truly seeking to understand the other perspective.

Try to populate your social media feeds with sources representing a variety of perspectives—politically, culturally, geographically, racially, and so forth. Read international takes on your own nation's news. Listen to podcasts outside your comfort zone. Watch documentaries on streaming sites that provoke you to think *deeply* (even if not, in the end, *differently*) about some issue. Take advantage of the Internet's platforming of voices you might not otherwise have opportunities to hear. One way to love your digital neighbors is to listen to them, even if what they have to say is hard for you to hear. Remember, you don't have to fully agree with others online in order to glean *some* truth from their perspectives.

5. SHARE WHAT'S GOOD!

One of the blessings of the Internet and social media is the ability to easily *share* what we have personally found helpful, good, true, or beautiful. One of my favorite C. S. Lewis quotes comes from *Reflections on the Psalms*: "I think we delight to praise what we enjoy because the praise not merely expresses but completes the enjoyment; it is its appointed consummation."[4] Don't feel guilty about posting online about a movie or book you loved, or sharing a photo on Instagram of your spouse, child, backyard, or something else you found delightful. The public praising of these things is a key part of our enjoyment of them. If you love discovering good music, create playlists on Spotify and share them. If you love taking photos of beautiful architecture, post them on an Instagram account. If you loved a restaurant or stayed at an amazing hotel, share a glowing review online that might lead others to discover it. Use the Internet to turn what you love into something that blesses others, rather than turning what you hate into something that angers others.

What would happen if everyone started to use the Internet more to celebrate the good than to add to the noise with hateful tweets and trigger-happy rants? What would happen if we used our on-line platforms to praise others rather than for promoting our own views and signaling our own virtue? What if we spent more time online publicly honoring people we do know than publicly sham-ing people we don't?

Don't Abandon. Redeem.

We know the Internet and social media are often cesspools of spiritual bacteria. The downsides are indeed massive. That's why this space occupies the least vital section of the Wisdom Pyramid. But is the Internet irredeemable? Should we just burn it all down and start over, as if it's some flea-infested, condemned structure or a radioac-tive wasteland like Chernobyl? No. And this is especially true for Christians, who might be the *most* tempted to run for the analog hills in the Internet age. Like the leper colonies, Ebola-stricken na-tions, or plague-infested medieval cities where Christians risked their own health to bring healing to others, the Internet and social media desperately need people of light to *stay* rather than leave.

But this doesn't mean you shouldn't be careful. Go online with your full-body hazmat suit on. Take a flashlight. Stay alert to dangers, always mindful of the highly contagious nature of the sicknesses online. But don't abandon the sick. Don't leave these spaces to rot. Instead, find ways to heal, to redeem, to be light in the darkness. Promote sources of life and truth and wisdom—Scripture, the church, nature, books, beauty—in the online space. Encourage the online world to breathe fresher air offline, but do what you can to improve the air quality online. With what you say and do online, plant virtual flowers and trees instead of clear-cutting virtual forests. At a table ever more cluttered with fatty, sugary foods high in spiritual cholesterol and artificial flavors, offer something both delicious and nutritious.

Don't just inoculate yourself against the epistemological sickness of the online age. Do your part to find a cure.

DISCUSSION QUESTIONS

1. This chapter highlighted three positive ways the Internet and social media can be valuable for wisdom. Can you think of others?

2. It's okay—even advised!—to "miss out" on much of what happens online on any given day. But do you feel social pressure, or personal temptation, to be constantly "in the know?" How do you resist this?

3. What rhythms have you found that work well for regulating time spent online, both for yourself and for your family?

Chapter 10

WHAT WISDOM LOOKS LIKE

Everyone then who hears these words of mine and does them will be like a wise man who built his house on the rock. MATTHEW 7:24

TWO OF MY FAVORITE church songs are inspired by the parable of the wise and foolish builders in Matthew 7:24–27. The first is a Sunday school song for kids, where we sang (with hand motions!),

The wise man built his house upon the rock
And the rains came tumbling down . . .
The rains came down and the floods came up
And the house on the rock stood firm . . .

The foolish man built his house upon the sand
And the rains came tumbling down . . .
The rains came down and the floods came up
And the house on the sand went smash.[1]

The other song is Edward Mote's classic hymn, "My Hope Is Built on Nothing Less," where the refrain goes:

On Christ the Solid Rock I stand
All other ground is sinking sand.[2]

I cherish these songs because their point is simple and yet profound: a life flourishes when built on a solid foundation. It collapses when built on the wrong foundation. This is one of the key ideas of the Wisdom Pyramid. The right foundation doesn't make what stands above it irrelevant; it makes everything above it structurally sound. By contrast, the wrong foundation leads to destruction and grief. And this is our problem today: we've flipped the pyramid and made social media and the Internet—shifting sands if ever there were!—our base. But this is a recipe for disaster.

A life built on the right foundation, however, is well-proportioned, sturdy, and able to withstand the rain, winds, and erosion of life. It's a life marked by wisdom.

Three Marks of Wisdom

The first part of this book highlighted three tendencies of the information age that make us *un*wise: too much, too fast, too focused on *me*. The second part presented a paradigm for an information "diet" more conducive to wisdom and spiritual health. How might our lives look different if we took a paradigm like this seriously? What new and countercultural fruit would our lives bear? Here are three marks I expect you'd see:

1. DISCERNMENT IN A "TOO MUCH" WORLD

Unlike the person at an extravagant buffet who puts heaping spoonfuls of everything delicious-looking on his plate with an inability to bypass anything, the wise person uses self-control, knowing when the plate is sufficiently full. He makes an effort to choose a balanced array of food that will not make him queasy later.

In today's world of information gluttony, wisdom looks like *intention*— approaching the glut not haphazardly, but with a plan. Rather than being passive and pulled around by the cacophony of alluring voices of folly, beckoning us to veer off the straight path (Prov. 9:13–18), the wise man keeps his gaze fixed straight ahead, following the path of righteousness, not swerving to the left or the right (Prov. 4:25–27).

In today's world, wisdom looks like the discipline of spending more time turning the pages of Bibles than scrolling through social media feeds; immersing ourselves more in the serene spaces of nature than in the clanging cymbals of cable news; developing a hunger for the nutrients of a healthy, local church more than the teeth-rotting candy of online clicks. It looks like cultivating rhythms of healthy information intake: building one's day, one's week, one's life around the sources most likely to bring truth.

2. PATIENCE IN A "TOO FAST" WORLD

Unlike the person whose diet consists mostly of fast food, drive-thrus, and other "on the go" snacks—because speed and efficiency are the utmost values—the wise person favors a more patient pace. He knows what goes into his body is too important to consume haphazardly, so he takes the time to choose wisely. He eats slowly and savors, recognizing that nutritious food is often made and consumed at a slower pace.

In today's world of speedy information, wisdom looks like *patience*—a willingness to slow down and process things well rather than simply amassing information and experience as fast as you possibly can. Wisdom looks like going against the grain of the bite-sized, low-attention-span spirit of our age, opting instead for longer and deeper chunks. It looks like putting devices away when you're sitting in church or across the coffeeshop table from a friend. It looks like joyful contentment with being "out of the know," happily oblivious to the fourteen Twitter controversies that have come and gone over the span of a week.

Wisdom also looks like rest: naps, Sabbath, a quiet day at home with no task lists or push notifications. Wisdom is the confidence that God is always on, but we aren't. We are mortal creatures with significant limits. When we sleep, and when we die, the world carries on without us. Sleep is, in fact, practice for death. How genius it was of God to build this circadian rhythm into our wiring—a daily reminder of our frailty and mortality. When we lie down flat, eyes closed, we look like corpses. When we sleep we are in a mysterious realm between life and death—perfectly still and impressionable, in some ways more attentive than in waking life. God created rest and sleep for our wisdom. Embrace it! You may miss out on what's #Trending online, but that's okay. You'll be wiser for having slept through it.

3. HUMILITY IN A "TOO FOCUSED ON ME" WORLD

Unlike the person who eats only what looks appetizing to him, making dietary decisions based solely on his appetites and gut-level desires, the wise person listens to the expertise of others: waiters at restaurants, chefs, doctors, dieticians. He knows his tastes and preferences are fallible and often untrustworthy.

In today's hyper-individualized iWorld, wisdom looks like *humility*—a recognition that, as much as technology puts us at the center of all decisions, we are not the best or highest authority. Wisdom looks like an eager willingness to seek guidance from others; a healthy skepticism about your own instincts and proclivities. Proverbs 3:5–8 captures it better than I can:

> Trust in the LORD with all your heart,
>   and do not lean on your own understanding.

In all your ways acknowledge him,
   and he will make straight your paths.
Be not wise in your own eyes;
   fear the LORD, and turn away from evil.
It will be healing to your flesh
   and refreshment to your bones.

Wisdom is an intellectual humility neither *over*-confident in one's own grasp of truth, nor *under*-confident in the fact that God reveals truth. Wisdom is knowing that, as Packer puts it, "our own intellectual competence is not the test and measure of divine truth." He goes on:

It is not for us to stop believing because we lack understanding, or to postpone believing till we can get understanding, but to believe in order that we may understand; as Augustine said, "unless you believe, you will not understand." Faith first, sight afterwards, is God's order, not *vice versa;* and the proof of the sincerity of our faith is our willingness to have it so.[3]

Wisdom is the peace of this "willingness to have it so." Perhaps one of the reasons anxiety is on the rise is that the ubiquity of information constantly teases us with what we *could* know—could read, could watch, could learn—if we only had the time. But wisdom accepts that we can never know everything, and that's okay. We learn much, and delight in learning, but we joyfully accept that the fruit of infinite knowledge is not ours to eat.

Interlude: Wisdom Is Liberation

Wisdom is freeing precisely because it submits to authority outside the self. But in a world preoccupied with power dynamics—oppressors and oppressed, the hegemony, the patriarchy, intersectionality, cultural appropriation, and so forth—we are skeptical of this notion. And it's true that many human authorities *are* oppressive and not conducive to our flourishing. But that doesn't mean the very *idea* of authority should be dismissed.

At its best, external authority is for our *growth*, not our *repression*. Italian Catholic philosopher Augusto Del Noce observes that the etymological root of the word authority is about growth (*auctoritas* derives from *augere*, "to make grow," which is tied to the words *Augustus*, "he who makes grow"). This is in direct contrast to how authority is popularly viewed today: as a stifling barrier to growth.[4] Today's world has reframed freedom as a defense mechanism: a freedom "from" rather than a freedom "to." We are "free," our society declares, insofar as we are subject to no external authority or objective reality outside the self. But is this really freedom?

Jesus did not say "total autonomy will set you free." He said *the truth* will set you free (John 8:32). True freedom is always hitched to truth—an objective, true-for-everyone truth that gloriously exists outside of our opinions, moods, and fickle temperaments. Without the truth, we are locked into a prison of our own making. But thanks be to God, the truth is out there and not in an abstract sense. It's there in the form of a person, Jesus Christ, who said "I am the way, and the truth, and the life" (John 14:6), and who calls every exhausted digital wanderer to sit at his feet and find rest:

> Come to me, all who labor and are heavy laden, and I will give you rest. Take my yoke upon you, and learn from me, for I am gentle and lowly in heart, and you will find rest for your souls. For my yoke is easy, and my burden is light. (Matt. 11:28–30)

Notice the equation here: "come to me" + "learn from me" = "you will find rest for your souls." If ever there was a simple equation for true freedom, it is this.

Three Orientations of Wisdom

It's significant that in Scripture, wisdom is often associated with a path. Are you going in the right direction? Are you veering off the path? Do you know where you are on the map? What's your compass? At the end of the day, wisdom is less about information than *orientation*. All the geographic data points in the world are useless if we have no sense of north. All of us wander in whichever nomadic direction our hearts choose, until we submit to the authority of God's good compass. He alone illuminates the path of wisdom. The fool says in his heart, "There is no God" (Ps. 14:1), and thus wanders aimlessly through the desert. The wise man, by contrast, lives a radically God-centered life. A. W. Tozer puts it this way:

> As the sailor locates his position on the sea by "shooting" the sun, so we may get our moral bearings by looking at God. We must begin with God. We are right when and only when we stand in a right position relative to God, and we are wrong so far and so long as we stand in any other position.[5]

As we conclude this book's reflection on wisdom, I want to look more closely at this "right position relative to God." What does this orientation look like? Perhaps the most important lesson of this book is that in order to understand what wisdom looks *like*, we have to understand *who* wisdom looks *to*, and listens to, and loves: "the King eternal, immortal, invisible, the only wise God" (1 Tim. 1:17 KJV).

1. LOOKING TO GOD

There is much to look at in life. Our eyes flutter back and forth faster than they can properly process. Wisdom is focusing our gaze on God: looking to him, praying to him, zealously seeking after him. The Psalms constantly reinforce this:

- "My eyes are ever toward the LORD" (Ps. 25:15).
- "For your steadfast love is before my eyes" (Ps. 26:3).
- "Those who look to him are radiant" (Ps. 34:5).
- "Our eyes look to the LORD our God" (Ps. 123:2).

The author of Hebrews calls us to "[look] to Jesus, the founder and perfecter of our faith" (Heb. 12:2).

Tozer describes faith as "the gaze of a soul upon a saving God . . . a redirecting of our sight, a getting out of the focus of our own vision and getting God into focus."[6] This orientation of sight is where wisdom, and life generally, thrive. Look to Jesus for peace instead of your circumstances. Look to Jesus for affirmation instead of Instagram. Look to Jesus for truth instead of yourself. Look to Jesus for wisdom before you look anywhere else.

2. LISTENING TO GOD

Wisdom is quieting ourselves in a noisy age and tuning our ears to God's speech through Scripture, his creation, and his church. Just as we are inundated with visual stimuli in today's world, so are we overwhelmed with voices beckoning us to hear their rant or sales pitch. What voices are we listening to? Are they trustworthy, consistent with the divine voice of wisdom (Proverbs 8)? This book has largely been about guiding us through this question.

Proverbs is constantly associating wisdom with *listening*:

- "A wise man listens to advice" (Prov. 12:15).
- "The ear that listens to life-giving reproof will dwell among the wise" (Prov. 15:31).
- "Listen to advice and accept instruction, that you may gain wisdom in the future" (Prov. 19:20).
- "Cease to hear instruction, my son, and you will stray from the words of knowledge" (Prov. 19:27).

Our age is unwise in large part because we are going deaf from the cacophony, losing our ability to listen well, if we listen at all. Wisdom means pressing mute on the voices speaking lies, and then opening our ears to the voice of God, listening intently to his every word. As Jesus said repeatedly: "He who has ears to hear, let him hear" (Matt. 11:15; 13:9, 43; Mark 4:9; Luke 8:8; 14:35).

3. LOVING GOD

Wisdom is not just intellectual knowledge *of* God. It's a deep longing *for* God. More than a desire to know the world *like* God, wisdom is the desire to know the world *with* God. Wisdom is a relentless pursuit of God's presence. It is a desperate hunger and thirst for God, the bread of life and living water. Wisdom is worship.

"Do not be content to have right ideas of the love of Christ in your mind unless you have a gracious taste of it in your heart," wrote John Owen. "Christ is the meat, the bread, the food provided by God for your soul."[7]

When I think of the wisest people I've encountered, one attribute they share is simply this: they love being with God. Their passion for God's presence is palpable in their joyful countenance and abiding peace. It's a look in their eyes when they taste a warm brownie, see a beautiful sunset, or hear a violinist play Vivaldi. It's not only the things themselves that bring a gleam to their eyes. It's who they see *through* them. They are tasting and seeing the Lord's goodness (Ps. 34:8). Because they love him above all other loves—all else in life makes sense. Existence becomes not only more bearable and more comprehensible. It becomes glorious.

Soli Deo Gloria

The life of wisdom is glorious because it is the way we were created to be. As our lives take on the shape of wisdom—rightly ordered and oriented around God—they naturally become more fully alive. And as they do, they bring glory to their Creator. Just as any thriving child brings glory to its parents, any bountiful vineyard brings glory to its vintner, or any verdant garden brings glory to its gardener, so do we bring glory to God when our lives manifest his wisdom. Our process of becoming wise is not for our glory, but for God's.

When we are *unwise*—feeding on a toxic diet that warps our minds and suffocates our souls—we become like a sickly, emaciated tree whose leaves are brown and whose fruit is rotten. We don't bring beauty and oxygen to the world; only blight and bitter fruit. Our roots are shriveled, our branches snap off easily, and the slightest wind could knock us down. We are like chaff.

But when we are *wise*—feeding on the bread of life (John 6:35), abiding in the vine (John 15:4–5), and drawing upon God-given sources of truth—we become like a robust tree planted near water (Ps. 1:3), with green leaves and vibrant fruit even when drought comes (Jer. 17:8). Our roots deepen securely into the ground, drawing life from vibrant streams. And our branches keep growing upward—like hands lifted in praise to their Creator. When the winds come—as they inevitably will, sometimes with furious force—these branches of wisdom won't break off. They will simply sway, as if clapping or dancing with joy, turning every storm into an opportunity to sing.

Soli Deo gloria.

DISCUSSION QUESTIONS

1. Who is the wisest person in your life? What characteristics about the person most demonstrates his or her wisdom?

2. If you were to rearrange the order of any sections of the Wisdom Pyramid, add another section, or take away a section, what would those changes be?

3. Can wisdom truly exist in someone who *doesn't* have any relationship to God? If so, how? What would that look like?

ACKNOWLEDGMENTS

A BOOK'S JOURNEY—like that of any created thing—is long and winding, with influences from countless directions along the way. In order of their appearance in this book's development, I'd like to thank: my parents, family, friends, pastors, and professors, who shaped my concept of and love for wisdom; my wife Kira for being a model of wisdom in our home; Thomas Terry and Ryan Lister at Humble Beast, whose invitation for me to speak on this topic sparked the idea of a Wisdom Pyramid; Jeremy Hamann for beautifully designing the original Wisdom Pyramid graphic; Matt Smethurst for giving the graphic much love on Twitter; Mandy Randolph, whose prophetic words at a church retreat confirmed my conviction to write the book; my agent Erik Wolgemuth for helping me initially process the idea as a book; Dave DeWit and others at Crossway for getting the project off the ground and seeing it through to completion; Jac La Tour, Jesse La Tour, Larry Sittig, Joshua Ryan Butler, and others who gave feedback on the book as I wrote it; the friendly baristas at Hidden House Coffee in Santa Ana, where I wrote the book; and my sweet boy Chet, who gave up his Saturday mornings with daddy for eight months so I could focus on writing.

NOTES

Introduction

1. "Word of the Year 2016," Oxford Languages, accessed April 9, 2020, https://en.oxforddictionaries.com/word-of-the-year/word-of-the-year-2016.

2. D. W. Pine, "Is Truth Dead? Behind the TIME Cover," *Time*, March 23, 2017, http://time.com/4709920/donald-trump-truth-time-cover/.

3. Jean M. Twenge, "Have Smartphones Destroyed a Generation?" *The Atlantic*, September 2017, https://www.theatlantic.com/magazine/archive/2017/09/has-the-smartphone-destroyed-a-generation/534198/.

4. Maggie Fox, "Major Depression on the Rise among Everyone, New Data Shows," *NBC News*, May 10, 2018, https://www.nbcnews.com/health/health-news/major-depression-rise-among-everyone-new-data-shows-n873146.

5. "Depression: Key Facts," World Health Organization, March 22, 2018, https://www.who.int/news-room/fact-sheets/detail/depression.

6. Dan Witters, "Record 21 States See Decline in Well-Being in 2017," *Gallup*, February 13, 2018, https://news.gallup.com/poll/226517/record-states-decline-2017.aspx.

7. *Cigna U.S. Loneliness Index: Survey of 20,000 Americans Examining Behaviors Driving Loneliness in the United States*, May 2018, https://www.multivu.com/players/English/8294451-cigna-us-loneliness-survey/docs/IndexReport_1524069371598-173525450.pdf.

8. "PM Launches Government's First Loneliness Strategy," Gov.UK, October 15, 2018, https://www.gov.uk/government/news/pm-launches-governments-first-loneliness-strategy.

9. Steven H. Woolf and Heidi Schoomaker, "Life Expectancy and Mortality Rates in the United States, 1959–2017," JAMA Network, November 26, 2019, https://jamanetwork.com/journals/jama/fullarticle/2756187.

10. Maryanne Wolf, *Reader, Come Home* (New York: Harper, 2018), 62.

11. This story is told beautifully in the documentary *Facing Darkness*, directed by Arthur Rasco (Samaritan's Purse, 2017).

Chapter 1: Information Gluttony

1. Jeff Desjardins, "What Happens in an Internet Minute in 2019?" Visual Capitalist, March 13, 2019, https://www.visualcapitalist.com/what-happens -in-an-internet-minute-in-2019/.

2. Jeff Desjardins, "How Much Data Is Generated Each Day?" Visual Capitalist, April 15, 2019, https://www.visualcapitalist.com/how-much-data-is -generated-each-day/.

3. Verlyn Klinkenborg, "Editorial Observer; Trying to Measure the Amount of Information That Humans Create," *The New York Times*, November 12, 2003, https://www.nytimes.com/2003/11/12/opinion/editorial-observer -trying-measure-amount-information-that-humans-create.html.

4. Quotes from Daniel Levitin in this section come from "Why the Modern World Is Bad for Your Brain," *The Guardian*, January 18, 2015, https:// www.theguardian.com/science/2015/jan/18/modern-world-bad-for-brain -daniel-j-levitin-organized-mind-information-overload, which is an excerpt from Daniel Levitin's book *The Organized Mind: Thinking Straight in the Age of Information Overload*.

5. Neil Postman, *Amusing Ourselves to Death* (New York: Penguin Books, 1985), 99.

6. Jacques Ellul, *The Technological Society* (New York: Alfred A. Knopf, 1964), 325.

7. Ellul, *The Technological Society*, 329.

8. Some of the content in this section is also published in my article, "How to Avoid Anger Overload in the Digital Age," *The Gospel Coalition*, July 15, 2019, https://www.thegospelcoalition.org/article/anger-overload-digital -age/.

9. Postman, *Amusing Ourselves to Death*, 68.

10. Postman, *Amusing Ourselves to Death*, 69.

11. Some of the material in this section comes from my article, "4 Ways Netflix Perpetuates Modern Anxieties," The Gospel Coalition, February 1, 2018, https://www.thegospelcoalition.org/article/4-ways-netflix-perpetuates -modern-anxieties/.

12. Alvin Toffler, *Future Shock* (New York: Random House, 1970).

13. Tony Reinke, *Competing Spectacles: Treasuring Christ in the Media Age* (Wheaton, IL: Crossway, 2019), 32–33.

14. Charles Taylor, *A Secular Age* (Cambridge, MA: The Belknap Press of Harvard University Press, 2007), 299.

15. Alan Noble, *Disruptive Witness: Speaking Truth in a Distracted Age* (Downers Grove, IL: InterVarsity Press, 2018), 24.
16. Maryanne Wolf, *Reader, Come Home* (New York: Harper, 2018), 198.
17. Jaron Lanier, *Ten Arguments for Deleting Your Social Media Accounts Right Now* (New York: Henry Holt & Company, 2018), 79–80.
18. I'm not suggesting this is actually the meaning (intended or not) of Apple's logo. It's just interesting to me that the ambiguous-yet-iconic logo might bring Genesis 3 and the "forbidden fruit" to mind.

Chapter 2: Perpetual Novelty

1. Rani Molla, "U.S. Internet Speeds Rose Nearly 40 Percent This Year," *Vox*, December 12, 2018, https://www.vox.com/2018/12/12/18134899/internet-broafband-faster-ookla.
2. Isla McKetta, "The World's Internet in 2018: Faster, Modernizing and Always On," Speedtest, December 10, 2018, https://www.speedtest.net/insights/blog/2018-internet-speeds-global/.
3. C. S. Lewis, *The Screwtape Letters* (New York: HarperOne, 1942), 137.
4. Nicholas Carr, *The Shallows: What the Internet Is Doing to Our Brains* (New York: W. W. Norton & Company, 2010), 193–94.
5. Maryanne Wolf, *Reader, Come Home* (New York: Harper, 2018), 72–73.
6. Carr, *The Shallows*, 138, 166.
7. C. S. Lewis, *Surprised by Joy* (Orlando, FL: Harcourt, 1955), 201.
8. Augusto Del Noce, "The Death of the Sacred" in *The Crisis of Modernity* (Montreal: McGill-Queen's University Press, 2014), 127.
9. Jonathan Haidt and Tobias Rose-Stockwell, "The Dark Psychology of Social Networks," *The Atlantic*, December 2019, https://www.theatlantic.com/magazine/archive/2019/12/social-media-democracy/600763/.
10. Tony Reinke, *Competing Spectacles* (Wheaton, IL: Crossway, 2019), 55–56.
11. Matthew B. Crawford, *The World Beyond Your Head* (New York: Farrar, Straus & Giroux, 2015), 16.
12. Erica Pandey, "Sean Parker: Facebook Was Designed to Exploit Human 'Vulnerability,'" *Axios*, November 9, 2017, https://www.axios.com/sean-parker-facebook-was-designed-to-exploit-human-vulnerability-151330 6782-6d18fa32-5438-4e60-af71-13d126b58e41.html.
13. Carr, *The Shallows*, 157.
14. Jon Levine, "Daily Beast Reporter Deletes 'Inaccurate' Tweets on Jussie Smollett Case," *The Wrap*, February 19, 2019, https://www.thewrap.com/daily-beast-reporter-deletes-inaccurate-tweets-jussie-smollett-case-trump/.

15. Kevin DeYoung, "Distinguishing Marks of a Quarrelsome Person," The Gospel Coalition, June 13, 2019, https://www.thegospelcoalition.org/blogs /kevin-deyoung/distinguishing-marks-quarrelsome-person/.

16. Jonathan Edwards, *Religious Affections*, ed. James M. Houston (Minneapolis: Bethany House, 1986), 147.

17. A. W. Tozer, *The Wisdom of God*, ed. James L. Snyder (Minneapolis: Bethany House, 2017), 164.

Chapter 3: "Look Within" Autonomy

1. Tom Nichols, *The Death of Expertise: The Campaign against Established Knowledge and Why It Matters* (Oxford: Oxford University Press, 2017).

2. "Kellyanne Conway: Press Secretary Sean Spicer Gave 'Alternative Facts'" *NBC News*, January 22, 2017, https://www.youtube.com/watch?v= VSrEEDQgFc8.

3. Abdu Murray, *Saving Truth: Finding Meaning & Clarity in a Post-Truth World* (Grand Rapids, MI: Zondervan, 2018), 14.

4. Alan Noble, *Disruptive Witness: Speaking Truth in a Distracted Age* (Downers Grove, IL: InterVarsity Press, 2018), 25.

5. Nancy Pearcey, *Love Thy Body* (Grand Rapids, MI: Baker, 2018), 21.

6. Pearcey, *Love Thy Body*, 32.

7. Family Policy Institute of Washington, "Gender Identity: Can a 5'9, White Guy Be a 6'5, Chinese Woman?" YouTube video, April 13, 2016, 4:13, https://www.youtube.com/watch?v=xfO1veFs6Ho.

8. "Read Oprah Winfrey's Golden Globes Speech," *The New York Times*, January 7, 2018, https://www.nytimes.com/2018/01/07/movies/oprah-winfrey -golden-globes-speech-transcript.html.

9. Alain Ehrenberg, *The Weariness of the Self: Diagnosing the History of Depression in the Contemporary Age* (Montreal: McGill-Queen's University Press, 2010), 218–19.

10. Matthew B. Crawford, *The World Beyond Your Head* (New York: Farrar, Straus & Giroux, 2015), 145.

Part Two Introduction

1. Peter Leithart, *Traces of the Trinity* (Grand Rapids, MI: Brazos Press, 2015), 10–11.

2. A. W. Tozer, *The Wisdom of God*, ed. James L. Snyder (Minneapolis: Bethany House, 2017), 65.

Chapter 4: The Bible

1. John M. Frame, *The Doctrine of the Word of God* (Phillipsburg, NJ: P&R, 2010), 56.

2. Jesus believed in the Old Testament (the Scripture he had at the time). It was "the foundation of Christ's whole ministry," argues Packer. "He challenged current interpretations of Scripture, but shared and endorsed the accepted view of its nature and status as an authoritative utterance of God." J. I. Packer, *"Fundamentalism" and the Word of God* (Grand Rapids, MI: Eerdmans, 1958), 58.

3. Packer, *"Fundamentalism" and the Word of God*, 139.

4. Packer, *"Fundamentalism" and the Word of God*, 161.

5. R. C. Sproul, *Scripture Alone: The Evangelical Doctrine* (Phillipsburg, NJ: P&R, 2005), 17.

6. Sproul, *Scripture Alone*, 85.

7. Westminster Confession of Faith (1.5), 1647, accessed August 25, 2020, https://www.ligonier.org/learn/articles/westminster-confession-faith/.

8. Frame, *The Doctrine of the Word of God*, 309.

9. Packer, *"Fundamentalism" and the Word of God*, 112.

10. John Calvin, *Institutes of the Christian Religion*, 1.7.4 (Peabody, MA: Hendrickson Publishers, 2008), 33.

11. Jonathan Edwards, *Religious Affections*, ed. James M. Houston (Minneapolis: Bethany House, 1986), 113.

12. Edwards, *Religious Affections*, 114–15.

13. Packer, *"Fundamentalism" and the Word of God*, 112.

14. There are many great books on the Bible out there, in addition to the ones I've already referenced in this chapter. Some you might explore for further reading on the nature, authority, and reliability of Scripture include: William Whitaker, *Disputations on Holy Scripture*; B. B. Warfield, *The Inspiration and Authority of the Bible*; D. A. Carson and John D. Woodbridge, eds., *Scripture and Truth*; Meredith Kline, *The Structure of Biblical Authority*; Michael Kruger, *Canon Revisited: Establishing the Origins and Authority of the New Testament Books*; Peter J. Williams, *Can We Trust the Gospels?*; Wayne Grudem, C. John Collins, Thomas R. Schreiner, eds., *Understanding Scripture: An Overview of the Bible's Origin, Reliability, and Meaning*.

15. When I worked in the marketing department of Biola University, I helped come up with the "Think Biblically about Everything" slogan and ad campaign. See "Biola University: Think Biblically. About Everything," YouTube video, February 28, 2013, https://www.youtube.com/watch?v=hdXwmOYBgSk.

16. Frame, *The Doctrine of the Word of God*, 165.

17. John Owen, *The Glory of Christ* (Edinburgh: Banner of Truth Trust, 1994), 33.

18. Augustine, *On Christian Doctrine* (Pickerington, OH: Beloved Publishing, 2014), 41, emphasis added.

19. Frame, *The Doctrine of the Word of God*, 296.

20. Matt Smethurst, "Does God Love You? You Own Tangible Evidence," The Gospel Coalition, July 22, 2019, https://www.thegospelcoalition.org/article /god-love-tangible-evidence/

21. John Wesley, preface to *Sermons on Several Occasions*, Volume I, accessed August 25, 2020, https://en.wikisource.org/wiki/Sermons_on_Several _Occasions/Volume_I/Preface.

22. Owen, *The Glory of Christ*, 158.

Chapter 5: The Church

1. C. S. Lewis, "Hamlet: The Prince or the Poem?" in *Selected Literary Essays*, ed. Walter Hooper (Cambridge: Cambridge University Press, 1969), 99.

2. Trevin Wax, "Why Is Expressive Individualism a Challenge for the Church?" The Gospel Coalition, October 18, 2018, https://www.thegospelcoalition .org/blogs/trevin-wax/expressive-individualism-challenge-church/.

3. Mark Sayers, *Reappearing Church* (Chicago: Moody Publishers, 2019), 187.

4. Benjamin B., "Emmanuel Lubezki, ASC, AMC Creates Emotionally Resonant Imagery for Terrence Malick's *The Tree of Life*," *American Cinematographer*, August 2011, https://theasc.com/ac_magazine/August2011 /TheTreeofLife/page1.html.

5. Lisa Respers France, "Chris Pratt Responds to Ellen Page's Claim His Church Is Anti-LGBT," *CNN*, February 12, 2019, https://www.cnn.com /2019/02/12/entertainment/chris-pratt-ellen-page-church/index.html.

Chapter 6: Nature

1. Dana Gioia, "In Chandler Country" (1986), Poetry Foundation, accessed April 9, 2020, https://www.poetryfoundation.org/poems/46412/in -chandler-country.

2. Cynthia Barnett, "Op-ed: We May Live in a Post-Truth Era, but Nature Does Not," *Los Angeles Times*, February 10, 2017, https://www.latimes.com /opinion/op-ed/la-oe-barnett-nature-alternative-facts-20170210-story.html.

3. Mark Evans, "Three Components of Wisdom," The Gospel Coalition, Canada Edition, June 13, 2018, https://ca.thegospelcoalition.org/article /three-components-of-wisdom/.

4. C. S. Lewis, "The Weight of Glory," in *The Weight of Glory and Other Addresses* (New York: Macmillan, 1949), 44.

5. John Calvin, *Institutes of the Christian Religion*, 1.14 (Peabody, MA: Hendrickson Publishers, 2008), 101.

6. Augustine quoted in Vernon Bourke, trans. *The Essential Augustine* (New American Library, 1964), 123.

7. John Frame, *Nature's Case for God* (Bellingham, WA: Lexham Press, 2018), 4, 7.

8. Jonathan Edwards, "Covenant of Redemption: Excellency of Christ," in *Jonathan Edwards: Representative Selections*, ed. Clarence H. Faust and Thomas H. Johnson (New York: Hill and Wang, 1962), 373–74.

9. Reginald Heber, "Holy, Holy, Holy," 1828.

10. Gerard Manley Hopkins, "God's Grandeur," Poetry Foundation website, accessed April 9, 2020, https://www.poetryfoundation.org/poems/44395/gods-grandeur.

11. Michael Horton, *Rediscovering the Holy Spirit* (Grand Rapids, MI: Zondervan, 2017), 48.

12. Pope Francis, *Encyclical on Climate Change & Inequality: On Care for Our Common Home* (Brooklyn: Melville House, 2015), 53.

13. Wendell Berry's poem "The Peace of Wild Things" is one of my favorites in a genre—nature poems—that is full of masterpieces.

14. Brett and Kay McKay, "A Call for a New Strenuous Age," *The Art of Manliness*, accessed August 25, 2020, https://www.artofmanliness.com/articles/call-new-strenuous-age/

15. Richard Louv, *Last Child in the Woods* (Chapel Hill, NC: Algonquin Books, 2005), 98.

16. Florence Williams, *The Nature Fix: Why Nature Makes Us Happier, Healthier, and More Creative* (New York: W. W. Norton & Company, 2017), 81.

17. Cassandra Brooklyn, "Forget Weed. Colorado's Hottest Trend is Forest Bathing," *The Daily Beast*, September 2, 2019, https://www.thedailybeast.com/forest-bathing-forget-weed-this-is-colorados-hot-mind-bending-trend.

18. Frame, *Nature's Case for God*, 82.

19. Pope Francis, *Encyclical on Climate Change & Inequality*, 57, 75.

20. Camille Paglia, "Camille Paglia: Feminists have abortion wrong, Trump and Hillary miscues highlight a frozen national debate," *Salon*, April 7, 2016, https://www.salon.com/2016/04/07/camille_paglia_feminists_have_abortion_wrong_trump_and_hillary_miscues_highlight_a_frozen_national_debate/.

21. Camille Paglia, "Feminism and Transgenderism," in *Provocations* (New York: Pantheon Books, 2018), 197–98.

22. Pope Francis, *Encyclical on Climate Change & Inequality*, 95–96.

23. Peter Kreeft quotes are from Humanum, "Episode 3: Understanding Man & Woman," Vimeo, 2016, https://vimeo.com/ondemand/humanum/161137718.

24. Some of this section is taken from my blog post, "Where Water Meets Rock," July 14, 2017, https://www.brettmccracken.com/blog/2017/7/13 /where-water-meets-rock.

25. Gavin Ortlund, "20 Reasons Why Christians Should Care for the Environment," *Soliloquium* (blog), March 8, 2008: https://gavinortlund.com /2008/03/08/20-reasons-why-christians-should-care-for-the-environment/.

26. Timothy Keller, "Lord of the Earth" (sermon, Redeemer Presbyterian Church, New York, NY, December 10, 2000), https://www.youtube.com /watch?v=BrbSET3IJS8.

27. Francis Schaeffer, *Pollution and the Death of Man* (Wheaton, IL: Tyndale, 1970), 91.

28. Francis of Assisi, "All Creatures of Our God and King," 1225.

Chapter 7: Books

1. Mark Edmundson, *Why Read?* (New York: Bloomsbury, 2004), 135.

2. Julianne Chiaet, "Novel Finding: Reading Literary Fiction Improves Empathy," *Scientific American*, October 4, 2013, https://www.scientific american.com/article/novel-finding-reading-literary-fiction-improves -empathy/.

3. Barack Obama and Marilynne Robinson, "President Obama & Marilynne Robinson: A Conversation—II," *The New York Review of Books*, November 19, 2015, https://www.nybooks.com/articles/2015/11/19/president-obama -marilynne-robinson-conversation-2/.

4. C. S. Lewis, *An Experiment in Criticism* (Cambridge: Cambridge University Press, 1961), 137–38.

5. Lewis, *An Experiment in Criticism.*

6. Susan Sontag quoted in Steve Wasserman, "Steve Wasserman on the Fate of Books after the Age of Print," *Truthdig*, March 5, 2010, https://www .truthdig.com/articles/steve-wasserman-on-the-fate-of-books-after-the-age -of-print/.

7. Marilynne Robinson, *When I Was a Child I Read Books* (New York: Farrar, Straus & Giroux, 2012), 23.

8. Maryanne Wolf, *Reader, Come Home* (New York: Harper, 2018), 56.

9. Andy Crouch, "On the News," 2020, accessed August 25, 2020, https:// andy-crouch.com/extras/on_the_news.

10. Edmundson, *Why Read?*, 135–36.

11. C. S. Lewis, preface to *On the Incarnation*, by St. Athanasius the Great of Alexandria (Yonkers, NY: St Vladimir's Seminary Press, 2011), 10.

12. Edmundson, *Why Read?*, 91.

13. Alan Jacobs, *The Pleasures of Reading in an Age of Distraction* (Oxford: Oxford University Press, 2011), 17, 23.
14. Augustine, *On Christian Doctrine*, 2.40 (Beloved Publishing, 2014), 80–81.
15. David Lyle Jeffrey, *Scripture and the English Poetic Imagination* (Grand Rapids, MI: Baker Academic, 2019), 215, 218.

Chapter 8: Beauty

1. Jonathan Edwards, *Ethical Writings* (1749), volume 8 of *The Works of Jonathan Edwards*, ed. Paul Ramsey, 550–51, Jonathan Edwards Center at Yale University website, http://edwards.yale.edu/archive?path=aHR0cDovL 2Vkd2FyZHMueWFsZS5lZHUvY2dpLWJpbi9uZXdwaGlsby9uYXZpZ 2F0ZS5wbD93amVtVvLjc=.
2. David Lyle Jeffrey, *Scripture and the English Poetic Imagination* (Grand Rapids, MI: Baker Academic, 2019), 10.
3. Jeffrey, *Scripture and the English Poetic Imagination*, 203.
4. Dorothy L. Sayers, *The Mind of the Maker* (New York: Harcourt, 1941), 22.
5. Richard Wilbur, "Lying," *Collected Poems 1943–2004* (Orlando, FL: Harcourt, 2004), 83.
6. Josef Pieper, *Only the Lover Sings: Art and Contemplation* (San Francisco: Ignatius Press, 1990), 32, emphasis added.
7. Cal Newport, *Digital Minimalism* (New York: Portfolio/Penguin, 2019), 103.
8. Matthew B. Crawford, *The World Beyond Your Head* (New York: Farrar, Straus & Giroux, 2015), 11, emphasis added.
9. Josef Pieper, *Leisure: The Basis of Culture* (San Francisco: Ignatius, 1963), 46.
10. Peter Scazzero, *Emotionally Healthy Spirituality* (Grand Rapids, MI: Zondervan, 2006), 143, 153.
11. Pieper, *Leisure*, 47, 48.

Chapter 9: The Internet and Social Media

1. Some of the material in this section is from my article "The Digital ~~Revolution~~ Reformation," The Gospel Coalition, November 19, 2019, https://www.thegospelcoalition.org/article/digital-revolution-reformation/.
2. Justin Earley, *The Common Rule* (Downers Grove, IL: IVP Books, 2019), 88, 89.
3. Cal Newport, *Digital Minimalism* (New York: Portfolio/Penguin, 2019), 28.
4. C. S. Lewis, *Reflections on the Psalms* (London: Collins, 1958), 81.

Chapter 10: What Wisdom Looks Like

1. Ann Omley, "The Wise Man and the Foolish Man" 1948.
2. Edward Mote, "My Hope Is Built on Nothing Less" 1834.

3. J. I. Packer, *Fundamentalism" and the Word of God* (Grand Rapids, MI: Eerdmans, 1958), 109.
4. Augusto Del Noce, "Authority versus Power," in *The Crisis of Modernity* (Montreal: McGill-Queen's University Press, 2014), 189–90.
5. A. W. Tozer, *The Pursuit of God* (Harrisburg, PA: Christian Publications), 101.
6. Tozer, *The Pursuit of God*, 89, 91.
7. John Owen, *The Glory of Christ* (Edinburgh: Banner of Truth Trust, 1994), 55–56.

GENERAL INDEX

SCRIPTURE INDEX

Also Available from Brett McCracken

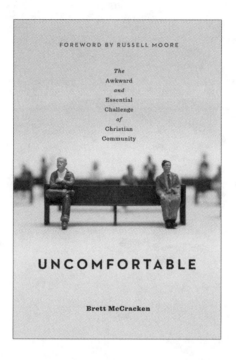

"In this book, Brett McCracken not only 'counts the cost' of life in Christ, but also shows why this uncomfortable life is also the most blessed."
MARK GALLI, Former Editor in Chief, *Christianity Today*

"Rather than retreating into a soothing world where everyone's 'just like me' or embracing the distractions of technology and consumerism, Brett McCracken calls us to life in community with God's people, where awkwardness, disappointment, and frustration are the norm."
MIKE COSPER, Founder and Director, Harbor Institute for Faith and Culture

For more information, visit **crossway.org**.